To dearest Philippa with fond love and happy memories

Michael

18th February 2006

Michael Olivier

A RESTAURATEUR REMEMBERS

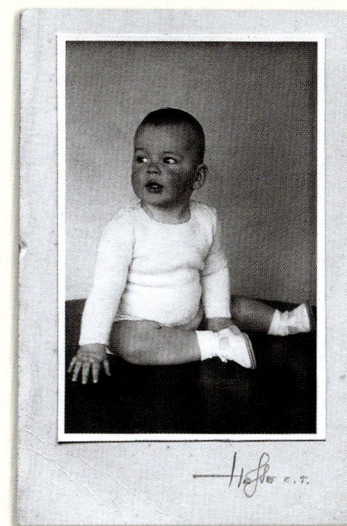

This book is dedicated with love to Madeleine,
Amy, Peter and Sarah

You are the sources of light around which I revolve.

And to Melvin – a great source of inspiration.
Thanks, Dad

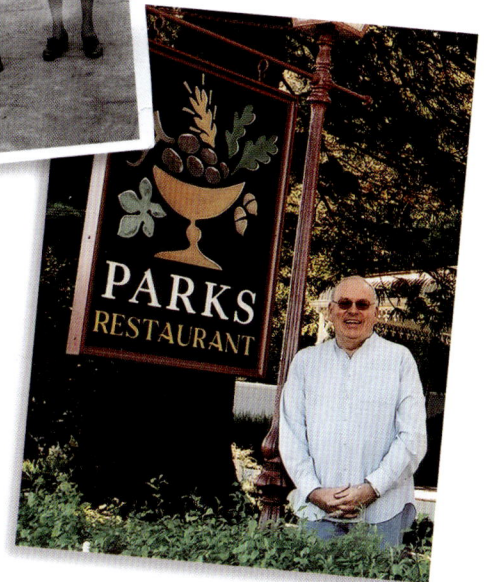

Michael Olivier

A RESTAURATEUR REMEMBERS

Me ...   7

Tea   17

Purple gallinules and pine nuts   26

Flapping pigs' ears and hot tripe   34

Summer Sundays   40

The pantry   51

Biltong and droëwors – an incurable addiction   60

Bobotie – quintessential Cape comfort food   66

Wine, autumn comfort food and olives   75

84 Wayside food

92 Lanzerac – my grand old lady

102 Paddagang – the Frog Passage

113 Parks Restaurant – us at our best

124 Maddy's food for boys

133 A miscellany of recipes

141 Acknowledgements

142 Index

CHAPTER ONE

Me ...

I GREW UP ON A WINE FARM at the bottom end of the African continent, with Table Mountain in my backyard. I grew up in a household that revolved around good food and good wine and wonderful music, from Satchmo to Saint-Saëns, Bach to Britten, Jussi Björling to Flanders & Swann and later on even The Beatles. And we had the most eclectic selection of literature, from Alan Paton to Adolf Hitler, Jane Austen to E M Forster and Ogden Nash to Shakespeare.

Conversation in the kitchen centred on the next meal or what was to be served for Saturday dinner or Sunday lunch, which was always a large meal with lots of family present and usually a couple of exotics who added much interest and intense amusement to our childhood. What sort of cake would there be? Would the mosbolletjies have risen enough to have them hot for tea or would we have to wait for supper? When would the olives be ready to pick and pickle? Were the gooseberries or the rhubarb or the Hanepoot grapes ripe yet?

There were always smells – smells from the kitchen of things baking, smells of trips to the sea, smells of the dairy, of fresh straw in the chicken run, the stables, the milking parlour and the smells of udder-warm milk, the sweetness of the frangipani and the gardenias, the nose-tickling smells of fermenting wine, the smell of ripe, sun-hot figs.

There were always tastes – crispy koeksisters pinched from a bowl of icy spicy syrup, yellow farm butter spread on hot, sour, potato-raised bread, 'cripsy' bits of roast lamb from the shank, the parson's nose of the chicken, crayfish we cooked on the beach and ate with mayonnaise, mushrooms from the lawn on toast.

There were always things to see from our farm, which was at the top of a hill now covered by a suburb called Durbanville Hills – the snow on the Hottentots Holland Mountains, the blue oceans that surround the Cape, boats in the harbour.

There were the sensations of season – the barely bearable heat of summer, which seemed to hang in the trees and rise up from the red dust in the yard, when the chickens would just sit open-mouthed and dogs would scratch sand patches under the trees to lie down in, the cool of the water in the farm dam, the marrow-freezing cold of winter on our knobbly, naked kneecaps after a snow-fall on the mountains, the warmth of the coal-fired Aga in the kitchen, the champagne mildness of late summer evenings and the crispness of the autumn mornings.

My brother Geoff and me.

There was always 'us' – my brother Geoff and me and, later, sisters Helen and Lilla. And there were the people who loved us – parents, grandparents, favourite uncles and aunts, godparents. And having parents who had divorced and remarried there was the confusion of more 'grandparents' and 'brothers and sisters', 'aunts and uncles' than most of our friends were used to.

Nevertheless, it was a childhood of enchantment. There was sadness too, of course, and a raft of other emotions, huge successes and some failures. But it set me up for an adulthood of huge fun. May this trip to the food, people and wine of my life be a fun one for you, too.

8

JOYCE GRENFELL – a talent to amuse me and the world greatly

I first met Joyce Grenfell when I was a young trainee at Lanzerac. I think it would have been in the summer of 1967. My first recollection of Joyce and her husband, Reggie, was in the dining room one evening. I was the stooge, so had to 'do' dinner duty. They sat next to Marie Rawdon, mother of the owner, who subsequently became a great friend of Joyce's. She too was a Christian Scientist and she and Joyce used to go to the CS Church in the Strand. One of the British dinner guests said to me, 'Do you know who that is? It's Joyce Grenfell!' I knew very well it was Mrs Grenfell because I had taken them to their table a couple of minutes before. But I was unmoved, because I was totally unaware of the legend before me.

We had no television in South Africa until 1975. Joyce Grenfell's radio programmes were never broadcast here, I never saw the St Trinian movies and I don't recall seeing any of Joyce's movies till after I met her. So I really first got to know them as a non-celebrity couple.

I like to think that I have a healthy sense of the ridiculous and as a result we hit it off immediately. She once asked me, 'Who is that gel who walks like a pony? Don't you think she has an amusing trot? That ponytail looks just like the tail of a horse at show jumping! And those high-heeled shoes!' The 'gel' was my Seychelloise dining-room manager. It was 1975 and by that time I was manager of Lanzerac.

Joyce was in South Africa launching *Joyce Grenfell Requests the Pleasure*. Gorry Bowes Taylor, a journalist friend of mine, came to interview her at the hotel. She brought a photographer with her and had a late breakfast with Joyce. Joyce was going through a stage of wearing a rather bulky cap which she had on that morning. She and Gorry chatted away and the photographer took some shots. When he got back to the studio at the newspaper's offices, he developed the film and there was Joyce with a huge black crumb between her front teeth from some of the toasted brown bread she called 'Lanzerac porridge' she'd had for breakfast. There was much laughter, and another visit from the photographer fixed it. (When Joyce first appeared on Broadway, a critic mentioned in his review, 'Miss Grenfell has a set of teeth of which a horse would be proud.')

There was a real gem, a very *Gone with the Wind* chambermaid called Nellie, who looked after Joyce and Reggie. Nellie told me her father was an American sailor who 'come on a ship to Cape Town'. She was a bustler, a bit like a large Mrs Tiggy Winkle, who clucked and tutted and spoke the most perfectly pronounced English. She had been nanny to an English-speaking family in

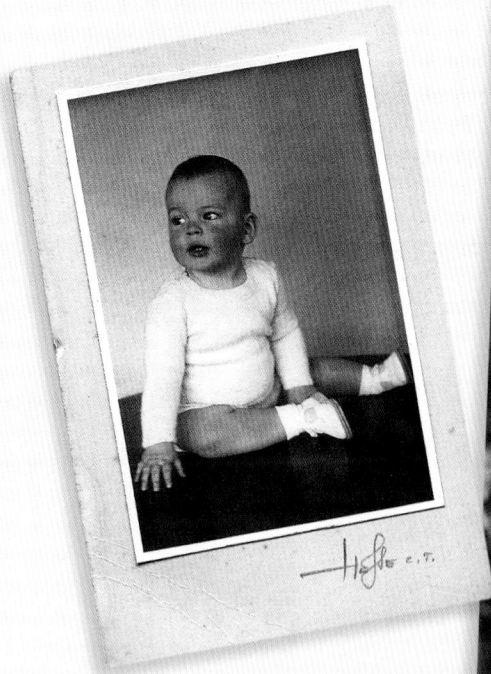

Above: Michael aged 9 months

Above: My grandfather
in the Parade Ring at the
Durbanville Gymkhana Club.

Above: My grandfather about to give my mother away,
to the tune of a Cape Town Highlander.

Above: Smoke break for Grandpa
at my christening.

Above: I can still feel
that beret on my head.

Above: My grandmother Trixie (front right) and my beloved aunts, (clockwise
from her) Freda, Edythe, Winifred, Doris, Maude and Florence.

Joyce at her flower table in Elm Park Gardens, London.

Stellenbosch before retiring and coming to work for us. She was always doing what she called her 'little favours for the ladies and gentlemen". She and Joyce got on like a house on fire. Joyce used to talk to her about Cliveden and the big houses she knew, and Nellie, having been 'in service', just lapped it all up.

Joyce was very opposed to the apartheid system. She spoke about it often, not in specific terms nor with any harshness or condemnation, but she knew it was wrong and that it couldn't last forever. She would not perform in South Africa for that reason. When being kind to people who asked why, she used to say that the British Musicians Union would not let Bill Blezard play for her here – which I am sure was true – and she simply couldn't perform without him.

They used to hire a huge car and we would drive down to the Strand in it to swim in the sea. 'The sea is so shallow here you have to go half way to India to get up to yer middle', she would say. We used to play on words a lot, so 'middle' became 'midhole', 'apple' became 'aphole', etc, which caused great giggles and Reggie's wonderful, mischievous, shy little laugh. She wore the strangest bathing cap, which looked a bit like a shower cap.

There were times when we went down to Gordon's Bay to have meals with my parents. My mother was a very good cook and they loved entertaining. I would drive the car because it was usually nighttime and Reggie wasn't too keen to drive in the dark. Joyce was not a good passenger and was always saying things like, 'You will drive carefully, won't you dear?' and 'Not too fast now!' One thing I will always remember about Joyce was her telling me that she liked to 'travel slowly and arrive early. It's just so restful don't you think?' I think this was a motto of hers about most appointments and times. At the end of supper, we would chatter away and one of us would say something that would get Joyce going and we would have our own little private cabaret. And it was here that I 'met' all her characters whom we came to know and love. Joyce was adept at using the South African accent, which is not one but many, and with her perfect ear she could mimic them perfectly. She would go on until we were dropping with laughter.

We would never include others outside the family because we never wanted her to feel that she was required to perform. Often, when driving back to Lanzerac, Joyce would sing songs for us, particularly Noel Coward's *I'll see you again,* which still brings tears to my eyes.

Spending an afternoon with them at their London flat, I felt very at home. I loved the John Ward watercolours that filled the walls, I loved the table with the little pots of flowers on it and I loved just being there with this amazingly special woman with her very special husband. I spent some other happy times with her. Once I walked with her down to the King's Road. She was greeted left and right by the barrow-boys and the shopkeepers, and as we approached them she would start imitating their accents under her breath and we would be in such a state of giggles by the time we got to them that I could hardly say 'Good morning'.

We got on a bus once in the King's Road and in Pont Street country Joyce started talking like a Sloane Ranger, about the weekend cottage and the 'hawsis' (horses) ridden by the 'gels'. This happened many times in different forms. There was a chap who sold flowers at Wellington Square in the King's Road. Fred's Barra it was called, and he just loved Joyce. 'Ello dahlin,' he would say to her and he'd get an 'Ello luv' back.

The last time we saw Joyce was at lunch at their flat in Elm Park Gardens in Chelsea. She and Reggie had just come back that morning from Aldeburgh – it was June 1979. They had stopped to pick some Suffolk strawberries on the way home, which we had for dessert. Maddy remembers it as being a delicious 'bits-and-pieces' lunch. I remember it being fun. Joyce had an eye patch on. 'Forgive me looking like a pirate, my darlings, but I'm dining with you-know-who at Windsor this evening and me eye needs a bit of a rest.' It was a very happy day.

In December that year she and Reggie celebrated their 50th wedding anniversary and the last time I spoke to her was the morning after The Party because we wanted to know all about it. She said she was very tired and that she would 'just stay in bed'. We didn't realise that she was dying and were devastated when we heard that she had passed away some days later. We were so thrilled that she knew the Queen was to bestow an honour on her and that she would be made a Dame in the New Year's Honours list of 1980. It was well deserved and I am so sad that she never had time to enjoy it. In the remaining years of Reggie's life we kept in contact with him and he always sent us the latest book or video that he had made. His death was the end of an era for us.

Because my food memory of Joyce is a strawberry one, perhaps a nutty version of Eton Mess might be appropriate, using meringues made from brown sugar.

NUTTY ETON MESS FOR JOYCE
Serves 6

You'll need:

125 ml each of whole blanched
   almonds and hazelnuts
375 g light brown sugar
6 large egg whites
½ tsp vanilla essence
about 300 g strawberries
port
balsamic vinegar
castor sugar
black pepper
500 ml fresh whipping cream
extra castor sugar and vanilla
   essence to taste
caramelised almonds for
   garnishing

Method: Preset the oven to 180 °C. Place the almonds and hazelnuts on a baking sheet and bake until fragrant and toasted, for about 8 minutes. Remove from the oven and cool completely. Rub the hazelnuts in a tea towel to remove the skins and chop both types of nuts roughly. Reduce the oven temperature to 100 °C.

Line two baking sheets with silicone paper or silicone mats and set aside. In the heatproof bowl of an electric mixer, combine the sugar and egg whites. Place over a pan of simmering water. Whisk until the sugar dissolves and the mixture is warm – for about 3 minutes. Transfer the bowl back to the mixer and fit a whisk. Starting on low speed and gradually increasing to high, whip until stiff, glossy peaks form – this will take about 5 minutes. Add the vanilla and mix to combine. Remove the whisk and fold in the nuts with a metal spoon. Spoon out the mixture in about 80 ml mounds onto the baking trays. Bake for one hour. Turn off the heat and dry out in the oven overnight. Cool the meringues and store between layers of paper in airtight containers for up to 3 days.

To prepare this pirouette of a pudding, you need a couple of hours for the strawberries to marinate. Wash them, take off the green tops and cut them in half. Place in a glass dish and splash over some port and balsamic vinegar, a sifting of castor sugar and a small fine grind of black pepper. Pop them, covered, into the fridge. Meantime, whip some fresh cream into a soft peak and flavour with vanilla essence and castor sugar. Chop up the caramelised almonds. Gently crush some meringues. Just before you're ready to serve, mix together the meringues, strawberries and cream. Serve in a bowl-shaped glass or on a flat plate and sprinkle over the caramelised nuts.

Wine suggestion: This quintessentially English summer dish would be best served with a rich, sweet, noble late harvest. Tyrell Myburgh's Joostenberg Noble Late Harvest Chenin Blanc and Ken Forrester's 'T' would make a perfect match.

THE BERRIO CABERNET SAUVIGNON

Bruce Jack is a busy man, a man without vineyards but with plenty of partners who grow grapes with and for him, a man with an office on the front seat of his car from which he directs his 'beyond-the-edge growers' for whom 'daring to go further' is part of everyday life and who grow vines in areas where you need hair on your teeth. If it's the flat, windblown, scrubby fynbos at Elim, near Cape Agulhas, the southernmost tip of the African continent; if it's the edge of the Karoo semi-desert, at Prince Albert; if it's shiraz from a traditionally white-grape area like Tulbagh; if it's a vineyard above the snowline in the Swartberg, where ancient clones of shiraz produce scraggy bunches with lentil-sized super-concentrated grapes; if it's a vineyard tucked away in the foothills of the Perdeberg – you'll find Bruce and his partners there.

The *Berrio* was, we are told, the first ship to round the Cape of Good Hope in 1497. And it is on the farm of Francis Pratt, in the cool climate of Elim, that the cabernet sauvignon grapes for this wine are grown. There is a sauvignon blanc 'sister' to The Berrio Cabernet Sauvignon, crisp like a fine Granny Smith apple and green like a ripe English gooseberry, a sister with stature and an elegant presence that is felt in the long aftertaste.

But back to The Berrio Cabernet Sauvignon, which is served up with a splash of cabernet franc. To me it is the equivalent of drinking chocolaty red velvet – well-fruited, dark velvet, sprinkled with soft spices taken from a fragrant oak box, touched with minty eucalyptus and roadside wild fennel, flavoured with blackcurrant. It has a full, almost orchestral flourish, of juicy flavour and baby's-cheek-soft tannins, finely balanced like the scales of justice. Well, we like to think the scales of justice are finely balanced. And the flavour just stays and stays and stays.

Bruce also helped me put my first label onto a bottle. Michael Olivier Verjuice is made in Bruce's Flagstone Winery from shiraz grapes from Tulbagh. It has a delicate blush pink and is ready to be used to add great flair to food (says he in all modesty!).

15

Hermanus, with the Marine Hotel in the centre.

CHAPTER TWO

Tea ...

IN HER BOOK *The Art of Eating*, M F K Fisher said, 'The smell of good bread baking, like the sound of lightly flowing water, is indescribable in its evocation of innocence and delight ...'

Smell is such a powerful reminder of things past. I remember the smell of the steaming, brown river water of boyhood baths at The Marine Hotel in Hermanus. I remember so well the smell the river water gave to the strong stewed tea we drank as eager, on-holiday children. In the early mornings we went out to fetch cups of it from the chambermaids, who served it with rusks from a row of stone pots on creaking teak trolleys, their starched uniforms rustling as they moved. Cups and saucers, spoons, milk and sugar were on the bottom of the trolleys with the daily menus and hotel newsletter – the sea temperature was a very important notice – and the previous evening's *Cape Argus*. The morning's *Cape Times* arrived only later on the early railway buses. Hermanus is the only town in South Africa to have a railway station with no track.

I would shout 'Hello!' down over the balcony at the ghillies gathering outside, waiting for their customers to come out before breakfast, bait in their little baskets, rods at the ready. The ghillies would take the residents fishing off the cliff path – my grandfather and some of his old mates among them – to bring back yellow-bellied rock cod and other exotic-looking fish, which the chefs would fry up for breakfast. How I remember those buttery tranches of seafresh fish served with wedges of rough-skinned Cape lemons, usually after a plate of thick, yellow, maizemeal porridge with crunchy, brown Demerara sugar and cream 'because we were on holiday', rather than the usual warm milk we were used to, poured from a blue-and-white-striped Cornishware jug.

On holiday in Hermanus in 1950, where my love for the place and passion for the MG motor car started.

Afternoon teatime at home on the farm was a great sensory experience too. I know that some people's childhood memories are either of summer or winter, but I am lucky to have memories of both. Strange, though, that many of my food memories are of winter, and tea is one of them.

Maddy and I still have the large, rectangular, Indian beaten-brass tray on which the 'tea things' were carried to the sitting room in the afternoon. On it was a huge, dark-brown, stone Derbyware teapot with a light-brown ring round the bulge. To this day I am still convinced that tea tastes better from a brown teapot. Again, there was that strong, stewed-tea smell that came right through the heavy coir tea cosy and its starched, floral, embroidered, Madeiran cover. The tea – leaf not bags – was usually from the Mazzawattee Tea Co., of Cold Blow Lane, London. Sometimes though (and why do I think it was Saturdays?), listening to a rugby broadcast over a crackling radio, it was rooibos – rich, red, flavoursome pools of it. There was a heavy brown jug as well for the hot water – I have that too. When there was a visitor, the 'tea things' were usually green Hallsware. Most often, though, they were Cornishware with thick blue-and-white stripes. Close to hand, for those who preferred coffee in those pre-instant days, was a bottle of Camp Coffee Essence – 'Drink Camp, it's the best'. There was also a couple of Oxo cubes – 'It's meat and drink for you!' – for those requiring a little nourishing beef tea. Towards the end of the week, our flushed-cheeked padre came to talk about the hymns to be played by my grandmother for the Sunday services. He was a trencherman of note and by sheer chance he always seemed to arrive at teatime!

Things to eat always accompanied tea. Over weekends, there were nearly always koeksisters. The syrup was made on Friday nights and allowed to get really cold in the fridge overnight. On Saturday mornings we awoke to the crackling sounds of the risen dough plaits in the hot oil and the sissing they made as they hit and sucked in the ice-cold, clear, spiced syrup, which had lemon peel, cinnamon sticks and cloves in it.

There were scones, at times studded with fat raisins, served with a soft strawberry jam made from strawberries grown in old wine vats with holes drilled down the sides and a central pipe for watering – one of my father's more unusual inventions. There was also the rich yellow cream from our Jersey cow, Amaryllis, which needed only one or two whisks to thicken it.

And there was the cake. One of our favourites was called German Tart. The recipe in my grandmother's book tells that it was renamed Continental Tart during World War 2. It consisted of a buttery, almond shortbread, layered with sour apricot jam and a neat pattern of blanched almonds laid out on top.

Then there was the vibrantly yellow poundcake – colour courtesy of our own eggs and home-made butter. It was made from one pound of butter, one of sugar, one of eggs and one of flour, and baked in loaf tins. But it was the process of preparing the batter that took the time. Maggie, our housekeeper, did not approve of our newfangled Kenwood. She wanted to 'feel' the butter and sugar creaming together. She would let the butter stand out overnight, to get it to the right consistency. Ambient pantry-temperature eggs were always cracked into a tea cup and shells upturned on a saucer for the last dribble of white to run out, later to be added to the batter. Flour, baking powder and salt were sifted through a large sieve – twice. The whole lot was slowly stirred together and the batter was poured into a loaf tin lined with stiff, buttered, greaseproof paper with some lemon verbena leaves stuck to the bottom, the perfume of which rose up through the cake, gently scenting it during baking. Sometimes Maggie divided up the poundcake batter and flavoured one third with cocoa powder, coloured one third with cochineal, left the remainder plain and then spooned the batter into a Bundt pan, creating a marbled cake. She also made a mean cherry cake, somehow getting the cherries to remain afloat in the batter instead of all sinking to the bottom during the baking.

The Hermanus Fishing Coast and Golf Course.

Historical photo of Hermanus with The Marine Hotel in the foreground.

KOEKSISTERS, KOESISTERS OR BRAIDED CRULLERS
Makes 24 koeksisters

Cold syrup is one of the great secrets of the success of koeksisters. Even during use it should be surrounded with ice cubes so that the hot koeksisters will suck in the cinnamon and lemon syrup. The oil should be hot (180 °C), but not too hot, otherwise the koeksisters will be dark and hard on the outside and not properly cooked on the inside. Koeksisters – or, as some will have it, 'koe-sisters' – were originally from Batavia and are generally plaited. In Malay homes, though, they may be made with mashed potato, cooked in an oblong shape rather than being plaited and served rolled in coconut. These are called 'bollas'.

For the syrup, you'll need:
1 kg white sugar
500 ml water
4 pieces stick cinnamon of about 4 cm
   in length
6 whole cloves
6 allspice berries
2 pieces – thumb size – fresh green ginger,
   well bruised with a rolling pin
3 strips of lemon peel, 2 cm wide and 4 cm
   long
2 Tbs lemon juice
a pinch of salt
a knifepoint of cream of tartar
1 tsp glycerine – add just before dipping
   to give the koeksisters a shiny coat

For the koeksisters, you'll need:
500 g cake flour
4 tsp baking powder
1 tsp mixed spices
½ tsp salt
4 Tbs butter, frozen and cut into
   tiny squares
250 ml milk
125 ml buttermilk
sunflower oil for deep frying
desiccated coconut (optional)

20

Method: The day before, prepare the syrup. Combine all the ingredients, except for the glycerine, in a saucepan and heat gently while dissolving the sugar. When the sugar has dissolved, bring the mixture to the boil and boil for 5 minutes. Set aside and allow to cool. Leave the spices and peel in the syrup, and when sufficiently cold, pour the syrup into a glass bowl and place in the refrigerator overnight. Shortly before use, it can be placed in the deep freeze to get it really cold.

Now prepare the koeksisters. Have ready two slotted spoons, one for lifting the koeksisters out of the hot fat and another for putting them into and removing them from the syrup. This method prevents more hot oil than necessary getting into the cold syrup. Sift the flour, baking powder, spices and salt into the bowl of a food processor. Add the butter and pulse until the mixture resembles a coarse meal. Add the milk and buttermilk and pulse till the ingredients are combined. Turn out onto a floured board and knead gently until the mixture forms a soft dough. Divide the mixture in two, place in a bowl and cover with a damp tea towel. Set aside for 30 minutes to rest.

When you are ready to make the koeksisters, have ready a baking tray covered with greaseproof paper on which to place the raw koeksisters prior to frying. Have another similarly lined to place the koeksisters on once fried in the oil and another containing a cake rack on which to drain the koeksisters once they have been dipped into the syrup. Have ready a large bowl filled with ice into which you put the bowl with the strained syrup.

Pat one of the balls of dough out on a floured board into a rectangular shape about 2.5 cm thick. Using a floured rolling pin, roll it out into a rectangle 20 cm by 10 cm and about 1 cm thick. Cut the rectangle into 4 strips across the width and 6 strips across the height. This will give you 12 koeksisters. Cut each one lengthwise into 3 strips, leaving them joined across the top. Plait them, seal the ends with water and tuck them underneath. Place them on one lined baking tray and cover with the damp tea towel while you repeat the process with the other ball of dough.

In a deep, heavy saucepan, heat the oil to 180 °C and then fry the koeksisters 5 at a time, turning them from time to time with the slotted spoon to brown them evenly on both sides. Remove from the oil and drain off the excess oil on kitchen paper for a brief moment. While they are still hot, drop them into the syrup for about a minute. When ready, remove them with the slotted spoon, drain a moment and place them on the cake rack. Continue with this process until all the koeksisters have been fried and dipped in the syrup. Serve them warm, when they are at their best, or at room temperature.

GABRIELLE KERVELLA – a goat's-cheese legend in her lifetime

Gabrielle Kervella with some of her ladies.

When I first met Gabrielle Kervella and her partner, Alan Cockman, we were dining in a restaurant in Perth called Jackson's with mutual friend Peter Forrestal, Western Australia's leading wine writer and author, who'd brought along some pretty amazing wines. I felt sure that she was a diplomat, she spoke with a crossover accent and was very elegantly dressed. In fact, I was in the presence of a legend, Australia's iconic goat's-cheese maker. Since then, Gabrielle, Alan and I have become great friends and a highlight for me on a visit to Australia was a stay on their farm.

Gabrielle, who trailblazed the making of farmhouse goat's cheese in Australia, bought her farm in Gidgegannup in the Avon Hills north of Perth in 1984. Western Australia is very flat, but the view over the Avon Valley is quintessentially Australian – with lots of eucalyptus and indigenous flora.

She started making goat's cheese as a way to keep the farm and it developed into a lifestyle despite all odds, even the Department of Agriculture telling her she'd never make it. But she'd seen small farms succeeding at it in France where she had worked to hone her craft, and thought she'd emulate them.

She had to breed up her herd, using Swiss goats – which are high producing and long lactating – and Anglo Nubians – a Middle Eastern variety producing a high percentage of milk solids. She needed the vigour of a hybrid to cope with the extreme heat of summer, the peak production period. Her herd is now about 200 in size with slightly more than half being milked. 'I can't have the herd sitting in the shed sulking because it's too hot outside,' she says.

Farmhouse cheese reflects its terroir, as does a great wine, and Gabrielle's soils had to be remineralised, adding natural dolomite to release tightly bound minerals in the soil. Doing this to the barren Western Australian soils was a huge task for which Gabrielle brought in experts. Even from the beginning she farmed using the barest minimum of artificial fertilisers and herbicides, and by improving the mineral content of the soil this encouraged the natural grasses to take over and reduce the weed content. Having farmed organically, she has recently 'gone biodynamic', which Gabrielle maintains has made its mark on the taste and texture of the milk and therefore on the cheese. She has found that her customers really appreciate the biodynamic certification – and the numerous and well-deserved awards.

Life chez Kervella starts early in the morning with the milk goats being called into the milking parlour just after dawn. It is the start of a 15-hour day for Gabrielle and Alan, for whom cheese comes from the soul. While the goats are being milked, the staff chatter away at them soothingly – stress is known to alter the flavour of the milk.

She uses milk produced on her farm only, because 'the transporting of goat's milk actually changes its makeup'. Daily production at peak is usually about 40 kilograms of cheese. The magic starts with vegetarian rennet being added to the warm pasteurised milk, which forms the softest of white curds. The curd cheese is drained for a short period, lightly salted and then sold in jars. For the other cheeses the delicate curds are carefully ladled into special moulds to maintain the shape of the curd, and allowed to settle down with no weight applied.

The Kervella Fromage Frais is a fresh, soft curd cheese produced in small rounds. It can be eaten as is, or with fresh chopped herbs and nuts, or rolled in smoked sweet paprika or finely milled black peppercorns. The rounds are also delicious brushed with olive oil and grilled and served on crusty farmhouse bread.

Gabrielle's Pyramides Cendre (ash pyramids) are coated in edible culinary ash in the traditional French style. This assists in the maturing and holding quality of the cheese and helps neutralise its acidity. The cheese has a creamy texture and a nutty flavour, and is ready for consumption when about a week old.

The Chevre Affine is a little log, usually mature from about 14 days after it is made. It is coated like a Brie or Camembert with a *Penicillium* mould. Unlike a Brie or Camembert, though, this cheese remains firm in texture, its flavours filling the mouth with the classic goat's-milk flavour, a reflection of Gabrielle and Alan's great talent as goat's-cheese makers.

In South Africa, there are several producers of excellent goat's cheese. Charles Back, of Fairview in Paarl, is as innovative with his goat's cheese as he is with his wines and has a large herd and a cheesery which produces both cow's and goat's cheese. Tantinki in Oudtshoorn and Foxenburg are more artisanal and both make excellent examples of goat's cheese.

FRITTATA FOR GABRIELLE

Serves four as a starter with some chunks of crispy bread, or two as a supper dish with bread and a leaf salad containing some wild rocket.

The following recipe happened after a visit to the Constantia Cheesery, which is owned by Lindsay Madden and is well worth popping into on a Saturday morning. Among other cheeses, I had bought 150 g of fresh, soft goat's cheese in a log shape. As I was leaving, Lindsay gave me a bag of fresh baby broad beans from his vegetable garden. Having made frittatas at a cookery demonstration in Cape Town with the well-known British TV chef Alistair Little, I used his techniques and made up this recipe as a loving thought to Gabrielle Kervella.

You'll need:
250 g freshly podded baby broad beans (or substitute with fresh or frozen peas)
1 onion, thinly sliced
extra virgin olive oil
4 eggs
4 Tbs chopped fresh parsley
sea salt
freshly ground black pepper
150 g fresh, firm goat's cheese

Method: Bring a pot of lightly salted water to the boil and poach the beans for about 8 minutes. Drain the beans in a colander and allow to steam a short while to chase off extra moisture. Meantime, in a non-stick frying pan fry the onion in a generous amount of very hot olive oil until a good golden brown. This will add another dimension of flavour, so use a good oil like Kloovenburg or Maradadi. Beat the eggs and parsley with a whisk and season generously with sea salt and freshly ground black pepper. Slice the cheese into thick slices. Put the beans on top of the onions and season. Place the cheese slices on top of the beans. Pour over the egg mixture and cook, pulling in the edges as the egg starts to get firmer. Allow it to become quite golden brown underneath. Slice the frittata into about six slices and then carefully turn each slice over to brown on the other side. If you find it easier, you can pop the pan under a hot grill to cook the top.

Wine suggestion: A sauvignon blanc from Constantia would be appropriate – Steenberg hits the spot.

OAK VALLEY SAUVIGNON BLANC

The Kogelberg Biosphere Reserve in Elgin is home to a staggering array of flora indigenous to the Cape, the smallest and most diverse floral kingdom on the planet.

The Elgin Valley, about an hour's drive from Cape Town, is on a plateau surrounded by some amazingly beautiful steep-sided mountains. This cool-climate plateau is ideal for the cultivation of flowers, fruit and vines.

Oak Valley has an excellent name for flowers and is one of the largest providers of quality blooms to the trade in the Western Cape. We used to use their flowers in Parks Restaurant. The livestock division farms 400 Simmentaler breeding cows on grass pastures producing top-quality beef under completely natural grazing conditions without the introduction of hormones or growth stimulants, in line with modern consumer demands.

But more importantly, the terroir at Oak Valley is eminently suited to the production of distinctive, cool-climate wines. In summer, when the more traditional wine-growing areas of the Cape endure the most excessive heat, the Elgin Valley is cooled by southeasterly winds which bring a protective layer of cloud over the valley, thereby creating significantly lower daytime temperatures.

Anthony Rawbone Viljoen, Oak Valley's owner, had for some years provided grapes to some top-marque wine producers. In 2003, in a year that was notable for hail and wind damage to spring growth, he produced his first vintage of Oak Valley Sauvignon Blanc. And talk about making a splash! Using yeasts noted for their ability to bring out the best in sauvignon blanc and leaving the wine on the lees for four months, he turned out a wine of a delicate, golden-straw colour. Its tropical fruit nose of granadilla, ripe gooseberries, fruit pastilles and freshly cut green grass is followed by a full mouthfeel, a creamy mineral flavour and nuances of pink grapefruit. It's apple crisp and dry, harmonious, and the flavour lingers well.

All these wonderful flavours resulted in the wine being awarded the accolade of the best sauvignon blanc at the 2004 Juliet Cullinan Wine Festival in Johannesburg, an annual benchmark of Cape wines. Imagine what their reds will do when they come into the arena!

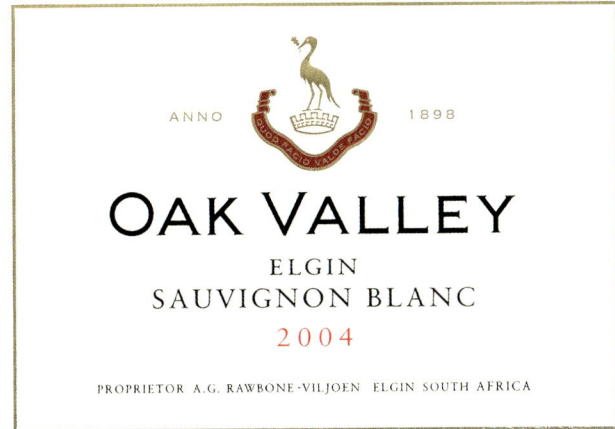

CHAPTER THREE

Purple gallinules and pine nuts

Provenance of the best eggs and great Sunday roasts.

'OH DEAR,' MY FATHER WOULD SAY in his deep, solid, slightly disappointed vicar's voice. And you never really knew what was coming. It could be 'We're out of Gentleman's Relish', or 'You haven't done very well in your exams, have you?' or perhaps 'No wonder I have a headache, we drank a whole bottle of Cherry Heering last night!' (he himself having pulled the cork and thrown it out of the window). But I think my favourite instance was standing by a farm dam once when he said, sotto voce, 'Oh dear, I've left my binoculars at home, and I think there is a *Porphyrio porphyrio* among the reeds over there, and now I'll never know!' We were very into zoological names, in the same way that the Cape ash at the bottom of the garden was always referred to as the *Ekebergia capensis*.

Birds played a very important part in our lives. We had a huge aviary filled with small South African birds. My brother and I had to leave the guinea fowl in the vineyards alone. They couldn't be shot 'because they eat the insects'. So we resorted to shooting rock pigeons instead, which quite often landed up casseroled in our own red wine, in the bottom oven of the Aga in the kitchen, for Sunday lunch. And *Roberts' Birds of Southern Africa* always accompanied us on long trips – with the binoculars! The farm chickens were very important too – for the pot and for their eggs. There was such a palaver on a Saturday as Dawid, the wheezy old gardener, would choose some poor unfortunate for a ritual beheading on the tree stump by the kitchen door, left there for the weekly execution. Sometimes, when he had been requested to choose two chickens, he would tuck the head of one of them under its wing and place the bird gently next to the stump while its friend was being dispatched with an axe.

Weaverbirds were such a part of summer. We had a polygamous Cape weaver named Solomon 'as he had so many wives', who used to build nests for his numerous partners in the row of stone pines behind the house. And the noise that went with it was deafening – weavers are no songbirds, they cackle. Weaver females are very choosy about their nests. Poor Solomon would take ages building one, nearly weaving blade of grass by blade of grass, and then introduce a wife to it. If it did not meet her approval, she would pull it apart and it would come thumping down on Dad's workshop roof. Solomon, poor soul, would start again. If the wife thought the nest passed muster, then she would take over the responsibility of the interior decorating. Sometimes, he would build a new nest on top of the frame of a rejected one.

Guinea fowl in the vineyards. We couldn't shoot them for Sunday lunch 'because they eat the insects'.

Apart from providing a peg off which to hang nests, the pines had another use too – they provided the means to make pitjie-tameletjies, or if you really want to be smart, pine nut and almond pralines. The Cape is covered in stone pines, the cones of which deliver what as children we used to call 'donnapits' (*dennepitte* being the Afrikaans word for 'pine nuts'). Quite often in pine-nut season my brother and I would sit on our haunches underneath the trees bashing open the hard covers of the pine nuts with two flat rocks and eating the sweet, fat nutmeats inside. Malay cooks of the Cape would use them with almonds to make sweets called 'kardoesies' which they wrapped in little squares of greaseproof paper (a 'kardoesie' is a little paper bag).

PITJIE-TAMELETJIES, PINENUT AND ALMOND PRALINES
Serves 6

You'll need:

250 ml water

2 cm fresh ginger

500 g white sugar

100 g pine nuts

50 g finely chopped almonds

12 lemon blossoms

a splash of orange blossom water

greaseproof paper cut into squares

Method: Bring the water to the boil, pour it over the ginger and allow to infuse for a while. In a frying pan, bring the water and sugar slowly to the boil, stirring to dissolve the sugar before the water boils. When the sugar mixture begins to caramelise, add the nuts and blossoms and continue cooking until it turns a rich, golden caramel. Stir in the orange-flower water and scoop little spoonfuls of the toffee mixture onto a non-stick baking sheet. Alternatively, simply pour the toffee onto the sheet and break it up into little bits when it is cold. When set and cold, wrap the pieces in the 'kardoesies'.

Serve after a meal, with coffee accompanied by a glass of Van der Hum, a Cape liqueur made from the skins of tangerines, or 'naartjies' as they are known. One of the best-kept secrets of the Cape is the variety of sweet muscadels available at excellent prices. One of my favourites is Domein Doornkraal Pinta, bristling with gold medals, a jerepigo made from pinotage and tinta barocca.

NORMA RATCLIFFE - Storm in a cellar

Twenty years ago, when people spoke of South African women in wine, the name Norma Ratcliffe was one of the first to come to mind. Today it still is. With her dynamic energy (I feel tired just being in her presence), she's been an expert at everything she's tackled – skiing, pottery, mountain-climbing and a raft of other things too, including 11 Argus cycle tours! In his book *Wines of South Africa*, Graham Knox gives a chapter to her, entitled 'Storm in a basin'. The basin is the bowl in which Warwick Wine Estate was established. The creator of the storm is Norma Ratcliffe, once met, never forgotten.

When Norma's late husband, Stan, bought the farm in 1964 – named Warwick by Colonel Gordon, Commander of the Warwickshire regiment during the Boer War – there was not a vine on the plot. Some 40 years later, the Warwick basin is the jewel in the centre of the crown of some of the greatest names in red wine in South Africa. Norma arrived at Warwick in 1971 as Stan's fiancée, and from that time the two of them started making experimental wines from early cabernet sauvignon vines he had planted. In 1980 they planted their first merlot and cabernet franc stock.

In 1985, Norma decided to go to Bordeaux for a harvest. She went to Château Sénéjac near Arsac, where New Zealander Jenny Dobson – now making pinotage in New Zealand – was winemaker. Shortly after Norma arrived there, Jenny broke her leg, so Norma had a baptism of fire in the cellar. 'I learnt', says Norma, 'all the tricks of the French cellar, how much people steal and all the tricks they got up to. And I even drove a mechanical harvester!'

Trips like these to Bordeaux, and lots of wine tasting, led to a decision to create their own winery and make wines in their beloved Bordeaux style. Stan, a genius with his hands, set about restoring the old winery and turning second-hand junk into usable winemaking equipment. 1984 saw the launch of a pilot project and the first wines under the Warwick label appeared in 1985. Stan died on May 21, 2004. Norma's son, Mike, is the third generation of Ratcliffes I have known and a capable pair of hands to take over the press at Warwick.

I once had an early-morning tasting with Norma of their wines – and what an experience that was! We started off with a tank sample of the 2003 Warwick Sauvignon Blanc, still in its milky youth, fresh and grapefruity, and later named for Professor Black. Her chardonnay is a new-oak fermented and matured wine, blended with tank-fermented wine. It's not a butter-brigade chardonnay, but has flavours of lovely citrus oil, and vanilla from the oak – a perfect, smooth blend. The very concentrated cabernet sauvignon is made from a new vineyard on high trellis on premium soils. It's very much a Bordeaux wine, with a cigar-box nose. The merlot is huge, powerful, meaty and intensely coloured – no gentle violets here, but excellent black chocolate and hot plum Tarte Tatin.

Norma was a pioneer of the single-variety bottling of cabernet franc, one of my hot favourite wines. I just love its damp forest-floor smells and sweet nose of fynbos followed by a rich, soft, mulberry taste. The Trilogy is Norma's flagship wine, with Karoo scrub on the nose and delicious ripe plums and berries on the palate. The Three Cape Ladies is a blend of pinotage, cabernet sauvignon and merlot with lots of sappy chewy fruit and a nutty crunch aftertaste, with an attractive label by Patricia Fraser. The Pinotage, bottled in a Burgundy-shaped bottle respecting its relationship with Burgundy, is Norma's 'new look' pinotage, with a little touch of oak in a soft fruity style.

I left Warwick after that tasting with such a feeling of being in the presence of a Good Success – the name of the original farm of which Warwick is now part.

Table Mountain in my backyard, constantly visible from our farm outside Durbanville.

CHICKEN BIRIANI FOR NORMA
Serves 6

Also spelt 'breyani' and 'beryani' in the Cape, biriani is Indian in origin but has been embraced in the Cape by the Muslim community as a dish of their own. This is a generous, festive dish. It was perfumed with saffron, though today, with saffron being an expensive item, turmeric is used instead to colour the rice. While Canada is Norma's land of birth, South Africa is her home, so I have restyled this dish for her.

You'll need:

400 g long-grained rice

2 litres water

1 Tbs salt

½ tsp turmeric

2 Tbs warm milk

4 medium onions – 3 of them sliced into rings and 1 chopped finely

4 cloves garlic, peeled and finely chopped

4 cm peeled fresh ginger

4 Tbs vegetable oil

6 Tbs seedless raisins or sultanas

6 Tbs slivered almonds

water

1½ kg skinned and boned chicken thighs, cut in half

250 ml yoghurt

For the spice mix, you'll need:

6 whole cloves

1 tsp cardamom seeds

2 tsp each whole cumin and coriander seeds

4 cm cinnamon

a good grating of nutmeg

½ tsp cayenne pepper

sea salt

freshly milled black pepper

For the garnish, you'll need:

3 hard-boiled eggs, peeled and quartered

fresh parsley or coriander leaves, chopped

Method: Wash the rice well, changing the water frequently. Place in a large bowl and pour over 2 litres of cold water and add the salt. Allow to stand for about 2 hours. This will keep the rice as white as possible and keep the grains separate. Dissolve the turmeric in the warm milk and set aside. Put the chopped onion, garlic and ginger with a little water into the bowl of a blender and process until you have a smooth paste. Set aside.

Put the oil into a heavy-bottomed casserole and fry the onion rings until they are brown and crisp. Drain on kitchen paper and set aside for the garnish. In the same casserole, using the same oil, repeat the process with the sultanas, frying them for a short while as they fatten up, and then fry the almonds until they are a light golden brown. Drain on kitchen paper and set aside.

Preset the oven to180 °C. Brown the chicken pieces all over in the same oil. Drain and set aside on kitchen paper. Add more oil to the casserole only if necessary. Add the onion-garlic-ginger paste and fry gently, adding a little water if necessary to prevent it sticking, until the paste takes on a light-brown colour. Add the yoghurt, a spoonful at a time, stirring well between each addition, and then place the chicken pieces on top of the yoghurt. Cover the casserole and bake in the pre-set oven for 30 minutes.

In the meantime, put the spices into a pestle and mortar and pound together or grind in a spice or coffee grinder until quite fine. When the chicken has simmered for 30 minutes, remove any oil from the top with a spoon or kitchen paper, sprinkle over the spice mixture, sea salt and freshly milled black pepper to taste, turn the chicken pieces over and bake, covered, for a further 30 minutes.

Meantime, rinse the rice again, boil in lots of well-salted water for six minutes, and drain well. Pile the rice in a pyramid on top of the chicken in the casserole. Dribble the turmeric milk down the sides. Sprinkle over a little of the browned onions. Cover closely with foil and the lid, and bake in the oven for a further 20 minutes.

When ready to serve, mix the chicken and the rice together gently with the chopped parsley or coriander and garnish with the remaining browned onions, the raisins and the almonds, and place the egg quarters decoratively on top. Serve with a green vegetable, such as shredded steamed cabbage flavoured with nutmeg.

Wine suggestion: This dish is perfectly partnered by Norma's Warwick Professor Black Sauvignon Blanc or the Warwick Chardonnay.

PAUL CLUVER GEWÜRZTRAMINER

Drinking Paul Cluver Gewürztraminer is like drinking spring rain. If you went out into the garden and collected gentle early morning rain from under honeysuckle, frangipani and Papa Meilland roses in full bloom, ran it over some ripe litchis and loquats, you would achieve more or less the same thing I am sure.

I am always happy to have this wine in my glass. It is a wine that is broad in flavour and the essence of all that is floral in scent and exotically aromatic and tasty in its fruit component. The conformation of the wine gives the impression of dryness, though it would be classed as off-dry. One of the more surprising accompaniments I had with it was a North African pastry called a B'stillah, which is filled with rice, chicken, quail, hard-boiled eggs, raisins and Christmas pudding spices like cinnamon and cloves – an exciting match. I have had the wine with soft Thai curries and with salmon and trout with a verjuice sauce. It is a wine you can drink on a Sunday morning in summer, with spiced nuts.

Elgin, the home of the Paul Cluver Estate, is one of the coolest wine-producing areas of the Cape. This area is fairly new in the history of wine production in South Africa, due to restrictions in the bad old days and very unnecessary control on where one could plant grapes. But now some of the better-known names in the industry are gently beating a path there to set up vineyards of their own. The Cluvers have an enormous piece of land, with tall elegant mountains bordering the farm on one side. It is almost Scottish in appearance, covered with scrubby, heatherlike, Cape fynbos. They are an environmentally-conscious family with the proclaimed intention of producing grapes in harmony with their surroundings. But they are socially conscious too, in that they have created an empowerment venture called Thandi with the local community. Thandi is well worth a visit. It contains a quaint and well-run restaurant serving Thandi wines made by Paul Kroukamp in the Cluver cellar under the guidance of Andries Burger (part of the family, since he is married to a Cluver daughter). Susan Kroukamp runs the restaurant and puts in appearances regularly at wine shows locally and internationally, peddling her wares in a most charming, educative way.

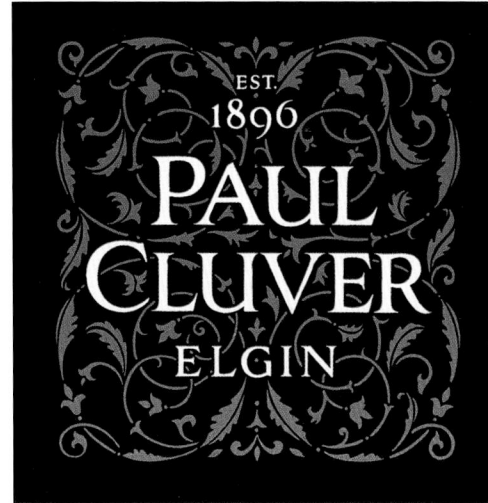

CHAPTER FOUR

Flapping pigs' ears and hot tripe

LET ME TELL YOU ABOUT TRIPE, flapping pigs' ears and sheep's trotters. Offal was such a part of my childhood, and yet to this day I cannot bring myself to eat tripe, even though Maddy just loves it. Other offal I don't mind. In my defence I can state that I have eaten a seriously delicious stuffed pig's trotter, which Pierre Kaufmann made so famous in London. Definitely a post nouvelle-cuisine dish, this is no child's portion arranged by an interior decorator. Brains, kidneys, liver and sweetbreads are fine – it's just the tripe thing I can't get into.

As a little boy, during the school holidays it was a big treat for my brother Geoff and me to travel with our father on Friday mornings to a meat packing co-op some miles away through the farmlands, to fetch weekly meat supplies. These farmlands are now covered in houses which form part of my worst architectural nightmare, constituting a suburb now called Brackenfell, a name I feel is more suited to a glen in the Scottish Highlands.

We had a blue, post-WW2, Ford pickup, the kind you now see being driven only by the likes of Clint Eastwood in movies such as *The Bridges of Madison County*. Sitting in the back on jute sacks, in the icy cold of winter, with snow lying thick on the Simonsberg, was no joke. But we were warmed by each other's company and our matching, thick, Fair Isle jerseys knitted on our mother's knitting machine from leftover bits and bobs from her other, more fashionable garments. There was a certain freedom to being in the back, with the frozen wind blowing through our hair as we bounced along the thin tar strips that passed for roads. Old Oak Road was one of them, but when I drove down it the other day I counted six lanes. Nothing stays the same.

Mr Neville, who was in charge of the butcher shop, and Mr Matodes, who had a keen eye for a racehorse and a well-turned ankle, particularly when my mother accompanied us, weighed and wrapped our purchases in brown paper and stout brown string. Apart from the finer cuts of meat, like fillet and leg of lamb and other weekly requirements, like the sheep's liver always served with browned onions and a beetroot salad for Saturday lunch, we would travel home with eight pigs' heads – and their accompanying trotters – all lined up at the back end of the truck, right way up, gently resting on a row of sacks. There is something quite peculiar about looking at eight pigs' heads staring at you with firmly shut eyes, their ears flapping in the breeze. The pigs' heads would be given to the farm workers, who made what Mrs Beeton would have referred to as headcheese, a kind of brawn, which they ate for lunch with piccalilli on thick slices of bread in the vineyards. There was also the large brown paper parcel containing what was referred to as 'Dad's offal' and in the kitchen as 'Meneer se afval'. This consisted of a sheep's head sawn in half, four sheep's trotters (and an extra set of four), the tripe, liver, kidneys and – most important of all – the brains, usually four or five. When we were lucky, sweetbreads were included too.

On arriving home, Maggie, our housekeeper, would take the sheep's head and, usually while we were having lunch at the kitchen table, wash and clean the two halves. The teeth and all the nasal passages were brushed out with an old toothbrush specially reserved for the purpose. The trotters were scraped with a knife, with particular attention being paid to the cloven hoof. The head and the tripe would then be laid into the large, yellow, enamelled casserole that Maddy and I used until fairly recently, when it was well into its 50th year – together with onions, garlic and thyme, salt and freshly ground black pepper and a couple of bottles of William Tell cider from Elgin. She then made a thick luting paste from water and flour, to seal the lid onto the casserole, which then overnighted in the bottom oven of the large, cream, anthracite-driven Aga that stood in the farmstead kitchen. The following morning, usually when we were sitting having breakfast, the casserole would be removed from the oven and the hardset luting paste beaten off with a wooden mallet. Lid off, a glance at the contents, particularly the cloudy cooked eye staring sightlessly heavenwards, was enough to put me off eating offal for the rest of my life. My father used to say the eyes tasted like hot grapes ...

Fortunately, I am able to eat kidneys and liver and just love brains done in brown butter with capers, on soft mashed potato. On grander occasions, when we had supper in the dining room (a rare occasion for us children) and the Granny Smiths were ripe in the kitchen garden, they would be baked and puréed velvety smooth and deliciously sweetly tart. This purée would be served as an accompaniment to fried brains, with toast soldiers made from sweet sourdough.

SHEEP'S LIVER IN CAUL (LEWER IN NETVET)
Serves 6 as a starter portion

You'll need:

1 large onion, chopped

2 fat cloves garlic

1 chilli, not too hot, seeded
    and chopped

a little sunflower oil

1 sheep's liver, cleaned with all
    the pipes removed

one quarter of the liver's weight
    in suet or lamb fat

1 Tbs wine vinegar

1 Tbs Worcestershire sauce

2 eggs, beaten

1 Tbs each chopped parsley
    and thyme

1 Tbs flour

sea salt

freshly milled black pepper

1 sheep's caul

Method: Preheat the oven to 180 °C. In a saucepan over medium heat, fry the onion, garlic and chilli in a little sunflower oil until lightly browned. In the bowl of a food processor, chop fairly fine the liver with the suet or lamb fat. Add the onion mixture, vinegar, Worcestershire sauce, beaten eggs, herbs and flour, and season to taste with sea salt and freshly milled black pepper.

Now to make this up, you can choose to make small portions the size of an egg, called Karoo Muisies (mice), or bigger versions called Skilpadjies (tortoises). My beloved mother-in-law, Anne Whittal, makes a huge roundel of a thing called a Pofadder (puffadder). She used to cook it over coals, the smoke adding a further dimension of flavour. Cold, with some home-baked bread, it made a pâté that if eaten at a roadside hostelry in France would have been declared some of the greatest food ever eaten.

Spread the caul out on a board. Place the liver mixture on it, bring the edges together and turn over so that it stands on the seam. If you're feeling energetic, sew up with a needle and thread. Place in a roasting dish and pour some melted butter over it. Season with sea salt and freshly milled black pepper.

Bake for about an hour, until well browned – it's quite important for the caul to be crispy – and a needle stuck into it draws clear liquid to show it is cooked.

Wine suggestion: I think that a really good sweet wine, like a noble late harvest, is a great foil to this dish, especially if it has a good acidic edge to it, like the Fleur du Cap, all glacé apricots and pineapple, honey and citrus – beautifully balanced. Or Glen Carlou Pinot Noir, which is like velvet raspberry – taste it lightly chilled, shut your eyes, and you're in Burgundy.

FRANK SWAINSTON – Chatelain of Constantia Uitsig

Frank Swainston came to the Cape in 1993 after a successful career in his restaurant Trattoria Fiorentina, in Johannesburg.

In partnership with the owners of Constantia Uitsig, Dave and Marlene McCay, Frank opened Uitsig in the early half of 1993, bringing a whole new culinary experience to the Constantia Valley and to Cape Town. He brought with him from Johannesburg his pasta maker, Peter Hadebe – now senior sous-chef – who has worked with Frank for 28 years. He and his chef, Clayton Bell, have created a legend of success in the Constantia winelands over the last nearly 12 years. I shudder to think how many hundreds of restaurants have opened and closed in Cape Town during Uitsig's lifetime. As neighbouring restaurateurs we supported each other. Our restaurants were both very successful and popular and more often than not full, so we sent people to each other and kept each other's guests on our waiting lists.

I think that if I were allowed to use only one word as a descriptor for Frank it would be 'generous'. He is generous in his flavourings, generous in his portion sizes, generous in giving of himself to both his staff and his many guests. All this comes from a calmness of spirit and the confidence of knowing that what he is doing, he is doing well.

At a recent meal at Constantia Uitsig, Frank suggested that we had a small first course of home-made pasta with porcini mushrooms. This simple dish is positively redolent of the forest floors of the mushrooms' provenance. While his menu tends to more than nod to Italy and the northern edge of the Mediterranean, there's a touch of the Pacific Rim too, as in his spicy Thai soup. He probably moves more tripe than any house of parliament, with what Jos Baker describes in her *Top 100 Restaurants* guide as his 'masterly Trippa alla Fiorentina'.

Frank, I think, will be amused that I dedicate a dish to him that won for Parks a top restaurant dish award in a guide prepared by Tony Jackman some years ago. Game birds are a feature of Italian cuisine. We had our supply of birds from a hardworking farmer called Derek Snijders, who farmed virtually the only guinea fowl available to Cape restaurateurs and used to deliver his birds himself to his customers.

Frank waiting for guests to arrive. How lucky they were to be eating his amazing food!

ROAST GUINEA FOWL WITH CÈPES RISOTTO
Serves 4

You'll need:

2 guinea fowl, cleaned and legs
    removed

olive oil

mirepoix for braising, made from
    onion, carrot, celery and leek

125 ml red wine

125 ml port

sea salt

freshly milled black pepper

25 g dried cèpes (*Boletus edulis*)

50 g fresh cèpes or other
    mushrooms, pan-fried in
    a little olive oil

50 g butter

1 onion, finely chopped

100 g arborio rice

500 ml guinea fowl stock,
    or more if required (this is
    created as you make the dish)

25 g butter

finely grated Parmesan cheese

25 ml port

10 g fresh sage

20 g broad beans

10 g finely chopped Parma ham

extra fresh sage for garnish

Method: Brown the legs in an ovenproof casserole with lid, using a little olive oil. Remove and drain. Add a cup of mirepoix and sweat gently. Place the legs on top of the mirepoix and pour over the red wine and port. Season with sea salt and freshly milled black pepper. Cover and braise in the oven at 180 °C for up to 2 hours until very tender and the meat strips off the bone easily.

Drain off the braising liquid and vegetables, and set aside. Remove the meat from the bone and shred, cool and set aside. Carefully remove the breast, trim and set aside. Roast the guinea fowl carcasses at 180 °C until lightly brown, and then place in a large stockpot with about 12 litres of water, with the leg bones and their braising liquid. Bring to the boil, simmer and then reduce to about 1.5 litres. Put the stock aside. Meantime, put the dried cèpes in a bowl, pour 500 ml boiling water over them and allow to reconstitute. Drain, but keep the soaking water for later use. Chop them up as well as the fried cèpes or other mushrooms.

Now make the risotto. In a saucepan, heat some olive oil and add the butter. Add the onion and sweat gently until soft. Add the arborio rice and sweat until the rice is transparent and well heated through. Make the risotto using as much of the boiling stock as is required. About ¾ of the way through the cooking process, add the cèpes and the soaking liquid. When the risotto is cooked, stir in 25 g butter and the shredded leg meat. Season well and add a little finely grated fresh Parmesan cheese.

Brown the guinea-fowl breast on both sides in a small pan. Deglaze with the port and pour round a little guinea-fowl stock. Wet-roast, skin side down, in the oven for about 15-20 minutes. Remove from the oven, set breast aside but keep warm. Reduce the liquid in the pan and add the sage, broad beans and Parma ham. Season with freshly ground black pepper, taste for salt. For each serving, place a quarter of the risotto in a deep dinner plate, carve the breast in thick slices and place on top, skin side up. Pour round the ingredients of the pan and garnish with fresh sage.

Wine suggestion: Constantia Uitsig Cabernet Sauvignon Merlot. The wine is dignified and restrained with all the elements in perfect balance. Excellent flavour of ripe black berries and soft red plums wrapped in perfectly ripe tannins, with a mineral savour and long aftertaste.

CONSTANTIA UITSIG SEMILLON

There are many experiences to be had on the Constantia Uitsig estate, which is owned and so superbly operated by Dave and Marlene McCay. Three well-visited restaurants are to be found here – the casual, generous, Spaanschemat River Café with its wine shop, the fabulous Constantia Uitsig and La Colombe, which more times than I can remember has been nominated the finest restaurant in South Africa by *Business Day*, one of South Africa's leading financial papers. La Colombe is presided over by Franck Dangereux, one of the most passionate and committed chefs I have ever come across. Every single thing he does, every plate he presents, every dish he creates is done with passion. His book, *Feast*, says it all. The hotel at Constantia Uitsig, a supreme example of *rus in urbe*, is one of the best appointed and comfortable places I have ever stayed in.

André Rossouw is Uitsig's viticulturist. A quietly confident master of his craft, he produces superb grapes which are taken across the vineyards of Constantia and delivered to John Loubser at Steenberg Cellar. Andre is very much part of the winemaking processes for the estate.

Semillon, or *groendruif* as it was known in earlier days in the Cape where it was heavily planted, is made for Constantia. And made in Constantia it produces a much-lauded wine. This is a wine of immense dignity. It has a golden thread seamlessly running through the citrus oil and waxy lanolin nose, the luscious fruit and its accompanying acidity on the palate supported by excellent aromas of French oak. And does it last on the palate? You could almost taste it still after brushing your teeth the next morning!

There is a cricket pitch on Uitsig, testimony to Dave McCay's cricketing past, with a quaint Victorian pavilion which sports one of the best views over the Constantia mountains.

Any wine from Constantia Uitsig, accompanied by the thwack of leather against willow, will make you a happy hedonist.

CHAPTER FIVE

Summer Sundays

SUMMER SUNDAYS invariably meant rising early and going to church. My brother Geoff and I would dress up in our choirboy cassocks with frilled and starched white collars, to sing in the church choir. It was the same little Anglican All Saints Church in Durbanville in which I was baptised and where I was to be confirmed by Joost de Blank – the very controversial Archbishop of Cape Town. Imagine my disappointment when he sent a mere bishop along to do the job!

In the large farmhouse things happened from early every morning, Sunday or not. We were usually wakened by the current cockerel of the backyard greeting the rising sun or by the clanging of the steel milk buckets on the outward journey to the milking parlour. 'Parlour' is probably too grand a word for what we had; 'lean-to shelter' might be a better description. The inward journey was made with the buckets full of frothing milk to be poured into the waiting large enamel bowl. This had a piece of muslin stretched over the top to sieve out any stray bits of straw and the odd bug or two. There was something magical about a glass of that milk instead of a cup of tea in the early morning, the warmth and nutty sweetness of it. It changed flavours throughout the year, depending on what was growing on the land in winter and spring or what was being fed to the cows in summer and autumn, when the grass was dry and stood short and upright like our close-cropped, little-boy haircuts.

Our breakfast porridge was made from oats, maize or sorghum, and at times from whole wheat berries soaked in water and held in the cool oven of the Aga overnight, then put through a mincer in the morning. Rarely, as boys, did we have a 'cooked' breakfast. There were always thick slabs of home-made bread and farm butter and jam of some sort. In the grape season, Maggie used to make jam from the fat red and white muscat grapes, known locally as Hanepoot. She developed a technique of removing them from the stalks and then taking out the two pips from each grape with a bent paper clip. She would then toss the grapes into a bowl of salted water with thick slices of our rough-skinned lemons, to prevent them from browning. She would cook them on the Aga in a large pot with snow-white sugar, until they were reduced to a limpid and utterly delicious jelly, which was best eaten on toast with peanut butter. At other times, there might be a mulberry harvest, after which the berries would be soaked to remove all the creepy crawlies that floated to the top. The mulberry is one of the most sublime of all berry fruits. It has a sort of dusty, dark, robust quality to it that I think is one of my strongest childhood flavour memories. In adult years I used to soak them in gin! We made marmalade too, from our rough-skinned Cape lemons, which was almost sweet with a bitter edge to it and clear like a jewel.

Lunch preparations were made well in advance, especially if marinating was required. Virtually always on a Sunday there was family of one kind or another visiting, and any number of unusual eccentric friends. The one who stands out best in my memory was someone called Karl who had been to the South Pole Arctic Base, where he thought the kitchen was really hot at minus 4° C. He drove a Volkswagen Beetle which suffered from pre-ignition, and he used to chug up the driveway and then leave the car and walk up the lawn with it still chugging away for what seemed like an eternity. There was any number of academics called Mr Glossop or Miss Smythe or Madame. Madame was a deep-voiced, delicately mustachioed French woman and was quite forceful in greeting us only in French and saying endlessly, 'Repeat after me ...', in her efforts to get us at least to say, 'Bonjour, Madame, comment allez-vous?' There was also an American called Ron who was a rocket scientist from Buffalo, New York, who had a show at the Labia Theatre called *Rivers of Fire and Ice,* about lava flows and glaciers. There was Graham who played the Dame in an ice show at the Luxurama Theatre, who got a bit touchy and feely for me!

What was served for lunch varied. More often than not there was a bowl of snoek pâté served with brown bread, or perhaps some cold pickled fish, prepared Malay style in a curry sauce.

If it was to be a braai, David the gardener would be deputed to get a fire going early, made from old vine stumps, to ensure plenty of hot coals to cook all the provender from the kitchen. The coals were carted across the lawn in a creaking wheelbarrow, shedding burning bits, to the shade of a pair of Norfolk Island pines, where two half 44-gallon drums awaited them. Over these

Below: Dulce, at about the time she moved to Durbanville, in the 1920s..

Left: Geoff and me with our mother, Dulce, at 19 Wellington Road, Durbanville.

Left: Geoff and me in Darling Street.

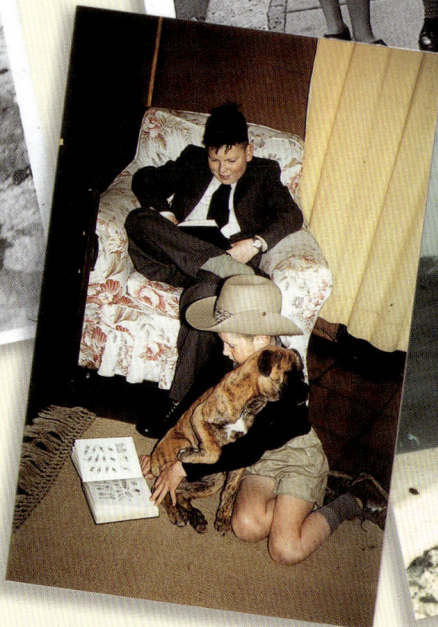

... and on Mouille Point Beach.

Above: Me in my SACS suit waiting to go back to boarding school. Geoff with Hector, our legendary Boxer.

Above: Lilla, Helen, Sarah Adonis and Maggie de Kock.

Left: Mom and me a couple
of months before she died in 1994.

Above: Helen and
Lilla cooling off.

Above: Taken in 1955 the year my grandmother died
and our lives changed forever.

Above: Geoff and me, boys no more.

coals would be cooked sosaties – curried, marinated kebabs made from chunks of fat mutton leg interspersed with pork fat, juicy dried apricots soaked in rooibos tea, onion wedges and *Pittosporum* or bay leaves. Then there would be butterflied legs of mutton marinated like venison, apple-, gherkin- and caper-stuffed double pork chops sewn down the side, whole fillets of beef which I recall my mother buying from a Danish butcher for 'only 97c a pound', and potatoes wrapped in foil, placed in the coals.

Sometimes lunch would be the traditional Sunday roast, either mutton legs with rosemary and onions, served with a rich gravy and mint sauce (though my brother Geoff would have apple jelly every time), or pork with the skin crisply crackled and accompanied by a chunky, lemony, apple sauce. If we had been good with the gun, there might be red-wine-roasted rock pigeons or almond-and-sage-stuffed Muscovy ducks which seemed for the whole of my childhood to make sucking noises in the mud round a dripping tap in the yard (it was kept dripping to keep the aromatic mint around it green and growing).

There was always a large salad, in a wooden bowl given to my parents by a cousin on the day they went to see *Never on a Sunday*. Maddy and I use it still. The salad was a mixed affair with lettuce and fruit, generous sprinklings of our own olives, and more often than not a dressing containing chunks of blue cheese. Or it could be coleslaw with tart mayonnaise and crispy bacon bits. We sometimes had egg-fried rice as a side dish, which my mother had been taught to make in an enormous wok over fierce gas flames in my presence – aged about 8 – by a dear old Chinese man who owned the Nanking Restaurant in Paarden Eiland, an industrial part of Cape Town where I was introduced to real Chinese food.

The puddings of one's childhood aren't quite the same when you are an adult. There was always a large jug of thick, yellow, cold custard, thickened only with eggs and flavoured almond-like with peach leaves. And there was daffodil-yellow cream, so thick it needed a spoon. Cream was served on Sundays only, because during the rest of the week it was kept for butter. Some of my favourite puddings were snow pudding – a gelatine-set, egg-white mousse deeply flavoured with lemon; trifle, generously flavoured with Old Brown Sherry, a bottle of which was kept specially for it in the pantry; apfelstrudel with its crispy pastry and sour Granny Smith filling; and water ice, now rather grandly called 'sorbet' in restaurants. This last had to be crunchy, made in ice trays, not churned, and was flavoured either with orange or lemon or, in the short strawberry season of my childhood, with fat sweet red strawberries, grown under cover on beds of straw. Sometimes we had pumpkin fritters. It is a tradition in the country to allow your pumpkins to ripen on the vine – to wait for the vine to shrivel and dry out. Then the pumpkins – either the flat white ones or the large, round, blue Hubbard squash known as Herbert squash, behind our kitchen swingdoor – were placed on a flat low roof to lie and bake in the sun to dry out, leaving the flesh sweet and bright orange. The pumpkin fritters were cooked on a girdle and served with lemon wedges and castor sugar into which ground spices such as cinnamon, ginger and cloves had been sifted.

There was always a huge table spread under the tall *Pittosporum* trees and covered with a large white cloth. It was laid with the Danish silver that Madeleine and I use to this day, large starched white napkins, voluminous wine glasses and jugs of water tinkling with ice and slices of lemon. And many bottles of Nederburg Rosé Sec – a delicious dry rosé – for which we supplied some of the Hermitage grapes from the farm, in a tear-drop-shaped bottle carved like cutglass at the bottom.

After lunch we lay on the lawn, stuffed like ticks, on leather rugs and lots of fat cushions, while the smoke of the vine coals hung in the lower branches of the trees about us. At this time we were usually treated to music. We had a new hi-fi gramophone! And we played vinyl discs. It was here that my music education really took place. My father had such an eclectic taste in music. We were as likely to hear Stravinsky as we were Bach, David and Igor Oistrakh as Benny Goodman, Robert Donat as Alan Sherman, Dylan Thomas as Louis Armstrong. Benjamin Britten's *War Requiem* featured strong as did Italian operas sung by the likes of Victoria de los Angeles, Callas, Björling and Merrill, and *lieder* sung by Fischer-Dieskau and Elisabeth Schwarzkopf. Quite often there would be lecturers from the drama department of the University of Cape Town, and plays would be read or Dylan Thomas poems recited while an overfed uncle, having consumed his post-prandial port and smoked his cigar, would gently fall asleep and before too long would be flapping his lips about and making the most amazing snoring sounds. Grandmothers' and aunts' heads would drop forward in jerks in their deck chairs while they tried bravely and with limited success to stay awake. Dogs would lie among us all, legs akimbo and twitching, dreaming of chasing rabbits, and William our Siamese would approach, arch-backed, mewing softly and purring, begging for a stroke or a touch.

This gentle afternoon session would be ended only by the rattling of a tea tray and reluctant noises about getting on the road back to Cape Town.

SMOKED SNOEK PÂTÉ
Serves 6

Snoek is a very traditional fish in the Cape. It is a firm fish which is served in many different ways. When I was a boy, I remember fishermen on horsedrawn carts blowing tin fish horns to announce their presence in my grandmother's street in Mouille Point. Kalk Bay Harbour during a snoek run is a popular place to buy fresh fish. If you are lucky, the fisherman will fillet the fish for you. Curried snoek-head soup is a very popular dish, accompanied by much sucking of bones!

You'll need:
250 g smoked snoek (any smoked
   firm-fleshed fish can be used;
   angelfish is very successful)
150 ml sour cream
125 g soft butter
grated rind and juice of
   one lemon
freshly milled black pepper
4 spring onions, green part
   included, well washed and
   chopped
1 Tbs chopped capers

Method: Shred the snoek between your fingers and place in the bowl of a food processor. Add the sour cream, butter, lemon rind and juice. Season with freshly milled black pepper. Process till smooth. Stir in the spring onions and capers. Taste for seasoning and add more lemon juice or white wine vinegar and more freshly milled black pepper if required. The pâté can be packed into a china pot and covered in melted butter, or simply placed on a plate. It is usually served either with Melba toast or with wholewheat seed loaf and butter. In the winelands of the Cape, it is served with whole muscat grape jam (*korrelkonfyt*) in a limpid syrup.

Wine suggestion: You need a soft, yet fully flavoured white wine here. I would suggest a visit to the Helderberg for a taste of Ingwe Sauvignon Blanc or Danie Truter's Onderkloof Floreal.

PUMPKIN FRITTERS
Serves 6 people with 4 fritters each

Loved by the children of the Cape, pumpkin fritters can be rustled up at the last minute when unexpected guests arrive. If they are made with a well-ripened and dry pumpkin (or Hubbard or butternut squash) they are deliciously full flavoured and sweet. The fritters are traditionally served with wedges of rough-skinned Cape lemons and castor sugar flavoured with powdered spices.

You'll need:

60 g cake flour

1 generous tsp baking powder

a good pinch of salt

2 eggs, well beaten with
    a little milk

500 g pumpkin which has
    been peeled, steamed and
    finely mashed

a little butter for frying –
    usually applied to the girdle
    with butter paper

Method: Sift together the flour, baking powder and salt, twice. Beat the eggs and the milk well and strain. Place the pumpkin in a large bowl and beat in the flour mixture. Add the egg mixture and beat well. Add a little milk if the batter is too stiff.

To cook the fritters, you can use a frying pan, in which you heat a half-half mixture of butter and oil, or heat a girdle and apply a little butter to the surface with some butter paper or greaseproof paper. Place the batter in tablespoonfuls into the pan and fry gently until brown. Turn over and cook on the other side. Drain on absorbent paper and keep warm. Serve with the lemon wedges and cinnamon- and nutmeg-flavoured castor sugar.

Wine suggestion: Dewetshof Edeloes – *edel oes* means a 'noble harvest'. This is a gorgeous, sumptuous wine redolent of dried fruit, roasted pineapple, thick aromatic honey and a whack of apricot to cut the sweetness.

47

MARY-ANN SHEARER – helping people to vibrant health

I used to babysit Mary-Ann Shearer when she was about six years old. She was an enchanting, little, smiley-faced girl of whom I was very fond. I am told that they liked me because I always brought sweets with me and allowed them to jump on beds! Mary-Ann broke a mirror on my bicycle and for years felt guilty about it till we met up again and she realised that I had forgotten all about it!

We went our separate ways, but years later Maddy and I were to meet Mary-Ann again, with her husband Mark and their three enchanting daughters, Melissa, Marie-Claire and Meredith. And of course, Stephen, a tousle-haired blond and blue-eyed charmer of a three-year-old, who surely makes Mary-Ann contender for the title of youngest grandmother in South Africa.

Mary-Ann's years of bad health in early life forced her to find a way of living that would foster natural health and wellbeing. Studying nutrition and natural lifestyles for over a quarter of a century, she has developed a basic yet effective programme which has led to much-improved health and increased vitality in most people who follow it.

Mark and the girls were the first to benefit from Mary-Ann's programme, and then the need grew after many people starting consulting her. Her first book to outline the programme, *The Natural Way*, is now in its 15th reprint. Mary-Ann has since written four more books – *The Natural Way Recipe Books* 1 and 2, *Healthy Kids!* and *Perfect Weight*, each a bestseller helping thousands of people in South Africa and abroad. Working with the University of South Africa she has developed a Natural Health and Wellness Home Study Certificate Course.

Mary-Ann and Mark now have a successful business, with a wide range of products under their own label, 'Mary-Ann's'. They operate from their home in Stellenbosch and a warehouse nearby from where they distribute their products nationally into supermarket chains and speciality stores. The products, made specially for them, all fit perfectly into Mary-Ann's 'Natural Way' requirements, so you'll find them low in salt, containing real seasonings, no added fats, no MSG and no irradiated ingredients.

Mary-Ann has a regular newsletter and a great website, www.maryanns.com, that is well worth a visit.

Mary-Ann, still enchanting and smiley-faced and still writing books and turning the nation towards health.

BARLEY AND MUSHROOM CASSEROLE
Ingredients can be doubled to serve 8.

Finding a suitable recipe from my own collection for Mary-Ann that will fall into the eating style of The Natural Way is no easy feat, being as I am into hedonism in food! Having checked her Natural Way Food Combining Chart, I think this one meets the criteria.

You'll need:

olive oil

3 cloves garlic, finely chopped

2 medium-sized onions,
   finely chopped

3 thick slices fresh ginger,
   finely chopped

1 chilli, sliced (leave in the veins
   and seeds for extra heat)

2 sticks celery, sliced

1 red pepper, sliced

250 g button mushrooms,
   quartered

150 ml olive oil

300 g barley

750 ml hot vegetable stock

sea salt

freshly milled black pepper

chopped parsley

freshly grated Parmesan cheese

Method: Preheat the oven to 180 °C. In a frying pan, using a little olive oil, fry together the garlic, onions, ginger and chilli until they start to colour. Add the remaining vegetables and cook over high heat to drive off most of the moisture from the mushrooms. Heat the olive oil in a cast-iron casserole and when hot add the barley and cook over low heat until golden brown. Add the vegetables back to the barley, pour over half the hot stock, cover and cook in the preset oven at 180 °C for about 45 minutes. Remove from the oven, stir gently and add the remaining stock. Add sea salt if necessary and some freshly milled black pepper. Let stand for 15 minutes. Just before serving, sprinkle over some chopped parsley. Serve with lots of freshly grated Parmesan cheese and a green salad.

Wine suggestion: You want a cool white to go with this dish and I mean 'cool', as in trendy and different. David Nieuwoudt's Cederberg Bukettraube would be a great match, with lovely, spicy, herbal tones that will add to the 'rustic' flavours of this dish.

A FUSION OF FIVE NOBLE VARIETIES

DE TOREN

WINE OF ORIGIN COASTAL REGION

FUSION V
2002

De Toren Private Cellar
Polkadraai Road
Stellenbosch

1,5 litre   SOUTH AFRICA   14,5% Alc Vol

DE TOREN FUSION 5

It was through Mark and Mary-Ann Shearer that Maddy and I met Emil den Dulk, who came to wine-making later in his life than most. He and Sonette simply decided to make one of the best wines in the Cape, and with dedication and purpose went ahead and did it.

De Toren Fusion V is a blend of the five Bordeaux varieties – cabernet sauvignon, merlot, cabernet franc, petit verdot and malbec. Every year the blend varies, depending on the harvests in the particular vineyards.

To see this wine in a glass decanter is to see it as a deeply red and rich wine that has sucked up its very soul from the root-entangled earth. It is almost regal and you just know when you get to taste it that it is going to be one of those special wine experiences. It is a perfect sum of all its parts, yet the greater for it. Underneath the queenly presence of the main theme of the cabernet sauvignon is the beautiful layer of excellent French oak, the whole filled out by accompanying choruses of the other varieties and the soft ripe rich tannins. Flavours of plums, Christmas pudding and sappy black berries make the wine just cry out for roasted meat accompanied by a superb sauce and the company of loved ones. The second label from De Toren is Diversity – no less a great wine either.

CHAPTER SIX

The pantry

IN DAGBREEK, THE FARMHOUSE WHERE I GREW UP, all the internal doors of the house were thick, solid, dark-stained wood with shiny, rugby-ball-shaped brass handles about two thirds of the way up the panelled doors.

The pantry faced south, which meant that it was naturally a cool room. Its only window faced onto a narrow, tree-covered passageway between the house and the winery. The window was covered with gauze netting to keep out all the insects that would have flown in by night and by day. There was a single, shadeless light bulb which glowed dimly in the centre, surrounded by twirls of flypaper which Maggie used to warm up on top of the Aga before sending us up on a ladder to attach them to the very high ceiling with a drawing pin. 'Dark' is probably quite a good word to use for the pantry.

On the pelmet, built up like breeze blocks with as much space between them as possible, were cakes of blue laundry soap. The soap was bought in long bars about 40 cm in length. It was a green colour with large patches of blue, not unlike Roquefort cheese. Maggie used to cut the soap into little rectangular cakes which Geoff and I would build up in layers on the pelmet. Bath soap was treated in the same way, following the 'Maggie Principle' that if it was dry it lasted a longer time once in use.

There were shelves on one side of the room, closed off with netting-covered sliding doors. Behind these doors was paradise. On the upper shelves were row upon row of bottles filled with preserves – whole peaches, apricots, pears. There were also huge, thick, green bottles filled with dark marmalade made from Seville oranges, lemon jellies with thin strips of rind suspended in them, chunks of citron in limpid syrup, pickled kumquats and ruby-red quince jellies. Others were filled with home-cured olives, which lasted from one season to the next. Bottles of orange and lemon syrup stood side by side with bitter grapefruit syrup and dark-red prickly pear syrup which we used to pour over thick slices of bread baked crisp in the Aga oven.

Lower down were the baked goods that were about to be used – loaves of salt-rising fermented bread cooling down, girdle scones, cheese scones and a jam tart or two. On the waist-high shelf were large, square, enamel tins marked White Bread, Brown Bread, etc and smaller ones marked Beans or Samp. There were also tins containing a variety of pulses and seeds that found their way into the baked goods coming out of the Aga oven and the slow-steaming casseroles that cooked on top. White and brown sugar, and white and wholewheat flour were kept in bins on the floor, which had huge scoops in them to ladle into the set of balancing scales that stood at the ready for any baking task.

There was a huge pre-war refrigerator that throbbed against the one wall, with a door so heavy it almost needed two people to open and close it. It was here, among the other more normal contents of a family fridge, that the cream was kept for butter-making.

After milking, the large bowls of milk would be carried through to the pantry and allowed to stand on a marble slab for a couple of hours for the cream to rise to the top. Sometimes the milkman would be instructed to keep the last couple of pints taken from the cow separate from the rest, because Maggie maintained that this was 'the best for butter'. Milk always tasted different, depending on the season and what the cows were eating. Winter butter was pale in colour and summer butter was a real buttercup yellow. When our Jersey cow, Amaryllis, was not in milk the butter definitely tasted different. Cream was saved each day from the morning and evening milking and usually allowed to stand out of the fridge for the day in order that it would turn slightly sour. We

There were always preserves on the pantry shelf and picnic baslets for wayside food.

52

liked flavoursome butter in our house, not the tasteless, almost-white paste used by the mothers of our village friends. A little culture in the cream was not a bad thing and the cream would be kept for up to a week before churning.

Churning was a task Geoff and I actually quite enjoyed. All sorts of magic comes into play in churning – especially temperature. The cream had to be at the right temperature. Churning in summer was usually done in the cool of the early morning or in the evening, never in the heat of the day. The churn we used was a large steel contraption that had 'Husqvarna – Made in Sweden' emblazoned on the side. It was a large, ball-shaped, lidded machine that had a sling on the one side which was swung, revolving the ball while the paddles remained stationary inside. The cream would get thicker, which sometimes would take an eternity, and then eventually the butter would form. Maggie chanted all sorts of rhymes during churning. I can't really remember them, but I do remember 'Come, butter, Come!' Buttermilk would separate out at the point of turning. This treasure was drained from the churn by means of a little screw-off cap on the side and kept in the fridge for making pendulas (turnovers – see page 55) and a baked buttermilk pudding (if it was successfully secreted from my father).

The butter was then turned out onto a sloped wooden board and beaten with wooden paddles to remove the last drops of buttermilk that remained. The butter was rather richly flavoured from the culturing of the cream, so not too much salt needed to be added. I found the butter used by my friends in the village very salty and not too pronounced in the flavour department. The large yellow pile was then divided into one-pound portions and shaped into a brick with the paddles and pressed to remove as much liquid as possible. There can be fewer more pastoral tasks than paddling butter. The pats were then wrapped in greaseproof paper, then brown paper and tied up with fuzzy brown string and kept in the fridge. The odd pound was given to visitors, especially our cousins from the city for whom this was a great treat.

White enamelware for the butter, milk and other delights from the kitchen.

GRANNY NEL'S CHEESE SCONES
Makes 18 scones

Granny Nel, the mother of a lifelong friend of my mother, was an accomplished baker. Though she died in the 1960s I can still taste her cheese scones, the recipe for which lived on in our house for years. Greater flavour could be achieved by using a more matured cheddar cheese, not easy to find in the days of the very restrictive dairy practices in the middle years of the last century, but treasured when it was found.

You'll need:
1 egg
full-cream milk to make up
  to 250 ml
165 g flour
3 tsp baking powder
sea salt
375 g cold butter
375 g grated cheddar cheese
cayenne pepper for light dusting

Method: Heat the oven to 220 °C. Beat the egg well in a 250 ml measuring cup. Add sufficient full-cream milk to fill up to the 250 ml mark. Beat again. Prepare 18 shallow patty pans by buttering and flouring them, using extra butter and flour. Sift the flour twice with the baking powder and fine sea salt. Grate the butter and rub into the flour until the mixture resembles fresh breadcrumbs. Add the cheese and stir in the milk-and-egg mixture briefly to just mix all together. Spoon into the prepared patty pans. Bake quickly until light brown – about 8 to 10 minutes. When the scones are cool, dust with cayenne pepper.

MARY McPHERSON'S PENDULAS
Makes about 12 pendulas

'Pendula', I was told as a child, means 'turnover'. And the provenance? – my great-grandmother, Mary McPherson, a quite formidable lady and mother of 13, of whom I have a photograph showing her standing with my grandparents, Frank and Trixie Bond, on Muizenberg Beach in winter in a wind. For pendulas we used a girdle, a large round black disc with a handle, which fitted onto the plate of the Aga stove. Madeleine and I still use it – it works like a treat on a gas flame. Served warm and steaming, pendulas were made for soaking up farm butter and the honey that came from hives kept by a schoolteacher of mine under some flowering gums on the farm.

You'll need:

125 g plain flour
½ tsp castor sugar
½ tsp salt
1 tsp bicarbonate of soda
¾ tsp baking powder
1 egg
250 ml buttermilk
30 g melted butter

Method: Sift together the flour, castor sugar, salt, bicarbonate of soda and baking powder, twice. Beat the egg well and add the buttermilk. Add the dry ingredients slowly, beating well all the time. Stir in the melted butter and beat well. Allow to stand for 30 minutes, adding a bit more buttermilk if the batter is too thick. Drop spoonfuls onto a hot, lightly buttered, non-stick pan and cook until bubbles form on the top and the mixture sets. Turn over and cook on the other side. Keep warm in a tea towel and serve with butter and honey or cinnamon sugar and lemon juice.

Caution: If you're using a girdle, remember that it takes a while for the temperature of the girdle to settle down. Start at a lower temperature rather than a higher one.

INA PAARMAN, Serene Queen of Cuisine

Ted Paarman is the most 'fed-up' man in Cape Town. I know this because in Ina Paarman's *The Good Food Cookbook,* quite a few of the recipes are prefaced by a remark like, 'This is one of my husband's absolute favourites' (Apple Tart with Boiled Condensed Milk), or 'My husband is of Irish extract and this is one of his favourites' (Irish Mashed Potato with Cabbage).

She has the knack of making the most modern recipes sound like something from her grandmother's cookbook, like Upside-down Caramelised Tomato and Onion Tart and Guinea Fowl Casserole with Red Wine. Her food is nostalgic, filling, comfort food and there's no fuss and bother with its preparation – her Marinated Leg of Warthog uses Coke and marmalade, for instance ...

Ina has been a friend for 20 years and she's one of Cape Town's greatest foodies, a writer, an author, a teacher and a TV personality. Her eponymous products are on grocery shelves round the country and on many shelves overseas, too. These no-nonsense products contain no MSG, no preservatives and no colouring. When she's wanted good sundried tomatoes, she's gone out and sourced the best growers and taught them how best to dry the tomatoes. Educating her suppliers and teaching people about good food is important to her.

Klein Constantia,
home of the world-famous
Vin de Constance.

INA PAARMAN'S WHOLE FISH OVER HOT COALS
Serves 8

You'll need:

3 kg fish

butter

lemon juice

ripe tomatoes, peeled and sliced

sea salt

freshly milled black pepper

sugar

fresh sweet basil, chopped

onion, sliced and fried

fresh parsley, chopped

Method: You have to get the wine organised and then get the fire going well in advance. Get your timing right, because the fish will take an hour to cook. You'll need a whole fish of about 3 kg to serve to 8 people. You'll need a friendly fishmonger to butterfly the fish for you and remove the spine but leave the head and tail on. When you're ready, rub in some coarse sea salt which will firm up the fish. Then chill it well for an hour or so.

Now comes the fun part! Have ready some greaseproof paper – double sheet, not the waxed kind and not aluminium foil – and newspaper.

Spread lots of soft butter and lemon juice all over the skin side. Lay the fish skin-side down on the greaseproof paper. Down one side of the fish, spread a layer of tomatoes. Season well with sea salt and freshly milled black pepper, a touch of sugar to cut the acid of the tomatoes, and add chopped fresh sweet basil. Basil and tomatoes are like love and marriage, they go together. On top of the tomatoes add a layer of fried onion (Ina doesn't fry hers, but I like to!) and plenty of chopped fresh parsley. Fold the fish to cover the filling. Wrap the whole thing up like a parcel in the greaseproof paper. Then wrap the fish in three sheets of newspaper, tie it up with string and wet thoroughly under a tap.

Bury the fish in a hollow in the coals, and cover with hot coals as well. After an hour, the paper will be charred and blackened. Remove the bundle carefully and place on a clean sheet of newspaper. Remove the charred paper and you'll find, as you remove the greaseproof paper, that the skin comes away easily from the tender aromatic fish. Serve with a tomato-flavoured risotto, a crisp, green, well-dressed salad and some garlic bread which you can heat in the coals at the same time as you cook the fish. Yum, Ina, yum!

Wine suggestion: This fish needs a really sparky sauvignon blanc, like Vernon Cole's Ridgeback Sauvignon Blanc.

CURRIED EGGS FOR INA AND TED
Serves 4

Ina is so innovative and fresh in her approach to food, so versatile with her products. This dish is my homage to her – a dish so essentially Cape. I hope Ted is really fed up by it!

You'll need:

8 extra large eggs

3 onions, thinly sliced
  (1 for the garnish)

2 fat cloves garlic

4 Tbs sunflower oil

2 Tbs mild and fruity curry
  powder

1 x 400 ml tin coconut milk –
  don't use the 'lite' version

half a 400 g tin chopped peeled
  tomatoes, preferably Italian

1 Tbs chutney

1 Tbs soft brown sugar

juice of half a lemon

sea salt

freshly milled black pepper
  if required

4 Tbs sunflower oil

50 g whole almonds sliced in half

50 g sultanas

sprigs of flat-leafed parsley

cooked rice for serving

Method: Place the eggs in a saucepan, cover with water, bring to the boil and simmer for 10 minutes. Pour off the water, and immediately run cold water over the eggs while cracking the shells. Leave the water dribbling into the pot until the eggs are quite cold – this prevents a blue ring forming around the egg yolk. Remove the shells, place the eggs in a bowl and cover them with cold water.

Fry the slices of two of the onions and the garlic very slowly in 4 Tbs sunflower oil until soft and golden in colour. Add the curry powder and fry for about 2 minutes. Pour over the coconut milk and tomato, bring to the boil, reduce heat and simmer for 10-12 minutes. Add the chutney, brown sugar and lemon juice, and season with sea salt and freshly milled black pepper.

In the meantime, fry the remaining onion in the oil until well browned, almost crisp. Remove carefully from the oil and drain on kitchen paper. Fry the almonds till light brown and then follow with the sultanas, which will puff up, and then briefly fry the parsley – drain on kitchen paper and set all aside for the garnish.

When ready to serve, cut the eggs in half and heat them in the sauce. Place the rice on a platter and lay the eggs down the centre. Garnish with the onions, almonds and sultanas and sprigs of flat-leafed parsley.

Wine suggestion: A fresh, crisp chardonnay from Robertson – Danie de Wet Chardonnay Sur Lie. Danie has made such a name for himself as a chardonnay producer in South Africa and has been an important figure in promoting Robertson as a fine wine appellation.

KLEIN CONSTANTIA VIN DE CONSTANCE

One evening at Parks Restaurant, Dougie and Celia Jooste, who own Klein Constantia Estate in the verdant hills of Constantia, reserved a large table. As they arrived, Celia said to me, 'We have a little vial of medicine for you,' and I was presented with a small glass bottle with a richly coloured liquid in it, rather like a sample one would take to a horse doctor. What I had not realised was that earlier in the evening they had opened a bottle of Constantia wine which dated from the early 19th century, from the cellar of Paul Bouchard – and they had brought me the last drop.

I could not have tasted this icon wine of the Cape without offering some to Maddy. I took it home, and the next morning after taking the children to school I poured it into a tasting glass and we tasted it before breakfast. Now it is simply not possible to block out the provenance of a wine like this when you taste it. Just as if you were drinking from the Holy Grail, surely anything drunk from it would taste wondrous. But after two hundred years it was still alive and grapey and it was a huge privilege to have the opportunity to taste such an old wine.

This, after all, is the wine written about by Jane Austen, Dickens and Baudelaire and which enjoyed the patronage of some of the crowned heads of Europe, Napoleon among them while he was in exile on St Helena.

Vin de Constance is a naturally sweet wine made from Muscat de Frontignan grapes, not unlike Hanepoot. No one is quite sure where the word 'Hanepoot' comes from – its direct translation is 'cock's foot'. However, legend has it that it could be a corruption of 'honey pot', possibly a description used by workers on the Constantia farms.

The wine is redolent of fruit – flavours of roasted pineapple, dried apricots and sunbaked raisins – combined in a silken-textured, sherry-coloured liquid pierced with a rapier tip of acidity. The two or so years the wine spends in French oak add vanilla and toasted almond croissants to the already teetering pile of flavours.

A visit to the Cape could not be described as complete without a taste of Vin de Constance.

59

CHAPTER SEVEN

Biltong and droëwors – an incurable addiction

MY GRANDMOTHER USED TO CALL BILTONG 'BUM STRIPS'. She knew that *bil* is the Dutch name for 'buttock', from whence the good meat for biltong originates, and that *tong* was a 'tongue' or 'strip'. And though we tend to think of it as a South African invention, it's not, nor is it unique to our neck of the woods. 'Tassal' was made in Batavia and probably came here with the Dutch colonisers and the Javanese in the 18th century (the Malays have brought so much that is tasty, colourful and cultural to the Cape). 'Tasajo' is still made in the Caribbean, and 'carne seca' in South America. Native Americans used to make 'pemmican' – small, thin cakes of meat, fat and wild fruits, which were dried in the sun. Even the Vietnamese have a dish, Thit Bo Kho, made from grilled dried beef – their version being flavoured with ginger, chilli, fish sauce and soy sauce.

Droëwors – dried sausage – is made specially for drying and needs to have a lower percentage of fat than conventional fresh sausage, which is normally fried, grilled or barbecued. Pork fat – which leaves a fatty deposit on your palate – is not ideal. Traditionally, the sausage would have had beef or lamb's-tail fat in it (although there are not too many lambs with fat tails around these days). Like biltong, droëwors is quite traditionally flavoured with sea salt and freshly milled pepper, though cloves, nutmeg and brandy are sometimes added (a good disinfectant, brandy). And it should be quite thin so that when dried it snaps like a twig. It makes a great snack with a glass of wine – red, white or rosé, dry or sweet.

Maddy and I even made biltong in rain-sodden Cape Town one winter, using a clothes drier with a heater fan in it – and very successful it was too, even though we kept on tasting to check the dryness – a bit like tasting bottles of wine from a case only to find, when you have one bottle left, that it has just reached its peak. We used an old family recipe given to us by her brother, Richard. He has a biltong loft in his old house in Cradock in the Eastern Cape, which is filled each year with biltong and droëwors made from venison he has shot and half a young steer he buys from friends in the area.

I have sliced meat to make venison biltong, off a springbok shot by Oom Jan – my gentle giant of an uncle – who used a Mauser with which to dispatch it. Very First World War, a Mauser. Several of the buck had hung overnight in the barn in the freezing mid-winter Karoo air. So the most important equipment other than the knife was bowls of warm water to thaw out our freezing hands while we were taking off the skin and cutting up the meat!

Biltong is made very much by feel, and each person making it has their own little wrinkles. One thing on which all agree is that the meat has to be of the best quality – be it beef, venison or ostrich. Flavourants rarely move beyond brown sugar, roasted coriander seeds, fine salt and freshly milled black pepper. The clever clogs add chilli and all sorts of fancy non-traditional spices – and vinegar. Our

My daughter Amy with her lifelong friend, Anna Fitzgerald, who died in the tsunami in Thailand, in December 2004.

butcher friend, Stuart Bass, of Supermeat Market in Kenilworth, tells me the vinegar is most important. He flicks the outside of his biltong with vinegar. Anne, my mother-in-law, drags hers through vinegar before hanging. The purpose of this is to prevent too much weight loss.

Forget about deep-fried chilli biltong puffs, biltong cream-cheese logs, biltong muffins and all manner of made-up dishes for this delicacy. For Maddy (for whom biltong is an incurable addiction which surpasseth all understanding) and me, all biltong needs is the sharp little Château Laguiole knife in her handbag, which cuts it so thinly that, apart from the little sliver of fat down the one side, when held up to the light it shines like an opalescent ruby. It's best eaten on its own – but just heaven with sliced, soft, farm bread spread with yellow Jersey butter and the merest touch of West Coast sea salt.

Friends too suffer from this addiction. Visiting Nicky and Steve Fitzgerald in Johannesburg, the kitchen cupboards are full of biltong in the form of snap sticks, as well as sliced, chipped and thin dried sausage.

FRANS MALAN – wine pioneer

Kaapse Vonkel, meaning 'Cape Sparkle', originated on Simonsig Estate over 30 years ago and was the name given to the very first sparkling wine made by the classical champagne method in the winelands of the Cape by a great pioneer and innovator, Frans Malan. Frans was somewhat of an icon in the wine industry in the Cape. He, Neil Joubert of Spier and Spatz Sperling of Delheim founded the Stellenbosch Wine Route in the early 1970s. He was part of the wine establishment, yet fought the authorities tooth and nail when he felt he was right. In his retirement there must have been a great sense of satisfaction in the knowledge that his three sons, Pieter, Francois and Johan, were carrying into the new millennium the torch of innovation, attention to detail and perfection that was kindled by Frans and Liza over the past 40 plus years.

Frans Malan [left] and Dave Hughes at our Parks Restaurant celebrating the 30th anniversary of the first vintage of Kaapse Vonkel.

Our links with this family go back to 1977, when Maddy and I were first married and she worked on Simonsig Estate, taking visitors on cellar tours and showing them how Kaapse Vonkel was made, conducting tastings and selling wines. What fun we had on Saturdays at closing time with Frans, Liza and the winemakers, mopping up the tasting wines left over from a busy morning's trading. How things have changed from those rather folksy days! Simonsig is now a large, well-run business exporting to more than 20 countries, and most if not all of their wines get four and five stars in the wine guides. Comments like 'benchmark wine', 'distinctive', 'statuesque presence', 'not lagging here' and 'groundbreaker' could be applied to any of their wines. Yet the boys have not lost the touch of keeping their visitors happy, remaining grateful for their inheritance and humble in their task.

One of the blissful things about a Méthode Cap Classique (winespeak for good local bubbly, which may not be called champagne in South Africa) is that it is drinkable with almost everything and on its own. What fun I had once taking the top off the bottle of Simonsig Kaapse Vonkel with Johan Malan's brand-new sabre from Barcelona. This was how thirsty French cavalry officers did it and it's not as easy as it looks when Johan does it. You waste less, and it's a lot safer, taking the cork off in the conventional way. And you don't cut your lips on the neck of the bottle either!

Liza Malan was one of the founder members of the Stellenbosch Fynproewersgilde – a guild of food-loving and pioneering Stellenbosch wine women who founded the now-legendary Stellenbosch Wine and Food Festival. As a tribute to her I offer my version of a real Cape favourite.

BOONTJIESOP – BEAN SOUP FOR LIZA
Serves 6

Cass Abrahams – an authority on Cape Malay cooking – says in her book *The Culture & Cuisine of the Cape Malays,* 'There isn't a great variety of soups in the Cape Malay Cuisine … the same basic recipe is used and is named after the thickening agent: peas, beans or lentils.' This soup could originally have been brought to the Cape by settlers from the Netherlands, for whom the early Malays cooked.

For the vegetarian version, you'll need:

375 g dried sugar beans, water for soaking

1.5 litres extra water

3 Tbs sunflower oil

3 large onions, peeled and chopped

2 large leeks, plus a bit of the green tops, peeled and chopped

3 carrots, peeled and thickly sliced

3 turnips, peeled and thickly sliced

200 ml ripe tomatoes, skinned, chopped, drained

sea salt

freshly milled black pepper

½ tsp ground mace

knife point each of ground cloves, cayenne pepper, grated nutmeg and ground allspice

grated rind of 1 lemon – no pith

chopped parsley for garnish

1 small chilli, seeded and finely chopped, with seeds and veins left in if you want extra heat

The carnivores can add 1 kg beef shin or marrowbones sliced thinly and 125 g pork fat or bacon with rind, chopped.

Method: The day before, pick over the beans to eliminate any bad ones and stray stones, and soak overnight in plenty of cold water covered with a saucer to keep all the beans below the surface. The next day, drain the beans through a colander and discard the water.

In a heavy-bottomed pot, gently heat the oil and when hot fry the onions, leeks, carrots and turnips until soft and lightly browned. Be careful not to burn any of the vegetables. Remove from the oil and set on kitchen paper to drain. If using meat in the soup, gently fry in the oil (adding more if necessary) until lightly browned.

Add the beans to the pot, add the onion mixture, the tomatoes (and the meat and its juices, if used) and pour over the water. Season lightly with sea salt, freshly milled black pepper, mace, cloves, cayenne pepper, nutmeg and allspice. Bring to the boil and then lower the heat and simmer for 90 minutes or up to a further 30 minutes until the beans are soft. Remove any scum or foam from the top during the simmering.

Remove the beef or marrowbones, if using, and cut the meat into small pieces. Discard the bones – our Labrador, Sebastian, is always a happy recipient. Using a potato masher, mash the vegetables, or remove some of the vegetables to give some texture to the soup and blitz the remaining soup in a food processor. Add back the whole vegetables. Taste the soup for seasoning, adding more sea salt and freshly milled black pepper if required. Add the lemon rind, parsley and chilli and return to the heat to heat through thoroughly. Check for final seasoning and serve in hot bowls with wholewheat bread and butter.

Wine suggestion: Simonsig Redhill Pinotage, produced from 40-year-old vines carefully tended by Francois Malan, on a hill of red soil on the estate. It is a supremely complex wine with a raft of the very best of pinotage aromas and flavours and more never attributed to pinotage. It also has a superb touch of toasty oak introduced by winemaker Johan Malan, adding an extra taste dimension. The wonderful promise of the nose is more than fulfilled on the palate and ends with a long aftertaste.

ZANDVLIET KALKVELD SHIRAZ

I must proclaim a special interest here. I have planted a vine on the Kalkveld (*kalk* is Afrikaans for 'chalk') on Zandvliet. And it has a brass plaque on it, engraved with my name. It is a cabernet sauvignon vine, mind you, but I still feel a bit like the poem that goes something like 'there is a piece in a foreign field that is forever ...' – well, 'me.'

Zandvliet is near Ashton in the Robertson wine area known for its lime-rich soils. It is an excellent area for horse breeding, which was the successful occupation of Paul de Wet Snr, father of Zandvliet's current incumbents, Paul and Dan de Wet. Horses still feature, though wine is now a greater occupation on Zandvliet.

Traditionally, grapes were planted on the more fertile river-bank soils on the farm. Dan and Paul decided that the chalky and less fertile Enon soils on the hills would be more suitable for vines. Ancient soils covered in Jurassic ant heaps, Paul tells us.

But – to the wine. Zandvliet bottled the first estate shiraz back in the 1970s, elegantly labelled with the unique Cape Dutch manor house and a horse featuring on the label. The label is almost unchanged today. This original shiraz is still bottled from old existing vineyards and continues to be the favourite of many.

The Kalkveld Shiraz is a more recent addition to the range and comes in two forms – a syrah which is matured in American oak, and a shiraz which is matured in French oak – creating two very different styles of wine. The syrah has the deliciously sappy, vanilla undertones imparted to it by the American oak and is a more forward, friendly and approachable wine – rather like an enthusiastic puppy that makes you want to love it, a wine for more casual eating and meat off the barbecue. The shiraz matured in the French oak is a more dignified, elegant wine, one that wants to be taken more seriously. She wants a white tablecloth and well-polished silver. The oak is present but in a gentle, understated way, supporting the delicious mint and eucalyptus flavours with hints of spices and roasted, ripe, red plums.

Special wines are indeed produced from this place, Zandvliet. Paul and Dan are gentle, kind men who are focused and driven towards perfection – and if they ever achieved it, would look anew at the horizon and indeed beyond.

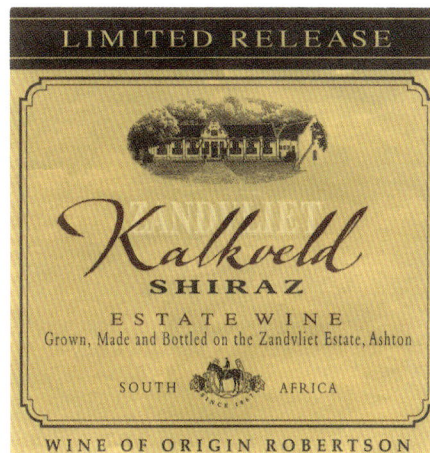

65

CHAPTER EIGHT

Bobotie – quintessential Cape comfort food

JAMES MICHENER WROTE A NOVEL which was very popular in the 1970s and 1980s, called *The Covenant*. Most Americans visiting our shores at the time had read the book before their visit and 'Have you read *The Covenant*?' was always the question they asked me. I was told of this brown earthenware dish that played such a major part in the book. It was handed down from generation to generation. And did I have the recipe for the dish that was served in it? How deep was my disappointment when I eventually read the book to find that the dish was actually a pudding I had never seen or heard of in all my years of being food aware. There I was thinking that at the very least it would be a bobotie.

Bobotie is probably one of the most widely known and best loved of all Cape dishes. It has its origins at the Cape in the 17th century, when Malay slaves, brought to the Cape by the Dutch settlers, introduced their unique style of cooking which was infused with the spices of the East. In the last century, it was made as a Monday supper dish from leftover lamb or beef (usually the remains of a Sunday roast). My favourite story about it was when King George VI was dining at the City Hall at a mayoral banquet, during the Royal Visit to South Africa in 1947. He asked what bobotie was, to be told by the lady guest seated next to him, 'Leftovers'.

In the South African home of today, raw ground beef is usually used. And if you want to bring tears to the eyes of a South African living abroad, bake and serve a dish of bobotie! Serve it with a selection of sambals, chutney (Mrs Ball's, if possible) and grated coconut, fresh if you can.

I had known of bobotie for years. When I worked at Lanzerac, the country-house hotel in Stellenbosch well known for its food and beautiful accommodation, Maria Jacobs – or Cookie as she was known – was the Bobotie Queen in the Lanzerac kitchen. She was immortalised in full technicolor by Laurens van der Post, well-known South African author, in the Time/Life book, *African Food.* Her bobotie was usually made from cold roasted meat left over from the lunchtime carvery roasts. Her innovations included putting whole hard-boiled eggs into the dish.

Cookie was a character in the major league. She was a large lady who dressed in the most voluminous pink overalls with matching bonnet and apron. Her large feet were always stuffed into a pair of towelling slippers several sizes too small. Some of her finest performances were given at 12h 30 when the hotel staff came in for their lunch, which it was her task to prepare. Of course she had her favourites, including some of her children and grandchildren, whom she fed well. But there were some members of staff she really disliked. I once saw her dish up a pile of samp (a sort of porridge made from whole, white-maize kernels), and on top of it delicately place a chicken neck. The recipient, understandably not charmed by this almost proteinless dish, simply upended it onto Cookie's head, turned on her heel and walked out, managing to control her tears till she was well out of Cookie's earshot!

Lanzerac, the beautiful, facing Table Mountain and the sunset.

MY BOBOTIE
Serves 6

You'll need:

1 thick slice white bread, crusts removed

250 ml cold milk

2 Tbs sunflower or peanut oil

1 Tbs butter

2 medium onions, finely chopped

2 fat cloves of garlic

2 Tbs medium aromatic curry powder

1 tsp turmeric

2 Tbs white wine vinegar

tamarind juice or lemon juice

1 kg ground beef (a portion of this could be ground fat mutton)

3 Tbs fruity chutney

50 g ground almonds

75 g unbleached seedless sultanas

1 Tbs natural brown or palm sugar

grated rind of one lemon and one orange (no pith)

4 bay leaves

sea salt

freshly milled black pepper

2 jumbo free-range eggs

knife point of turmeric (if desired)

6 fresh lemon leaves (for garnish)

Method: Soak the slices of bread in the cold milk, and when saturated, squeeze dry in a sieve and set aside. Reserve the milk to make the custard topping. Preset the oven to 180 °C. In a heavy saucepan, heat the oil and the butter. Start browning the onions over medium heat. After a while, add the garlic and continue cooking slowly until the mixture is a light golden brown. Add the curry powder, turmeric and white wine vinegar, tamarind or lemon juice. Cook for a few minutes to release the aromatic oils of the spices. Add the ground beef/lamb and stir with a spoon to break it up. Keep stirring until it loses its red colour. Add the chutney, almonds, sultanas, grated rinds, brown or palm sugar, bay leaves and seasoning. Add one of the eggs, beaten, and the soaked bread. Taste and season again if necessary. Pack into a flat ovenproof dish and smooth off the top. Cover and bake in the preset oven for 1½ hours. Turn down the oven temperature to 150 °C to cook the topping.

To make the topping, whisk the remaining egg into the milk, season, and strain if required. At this point you could add a knifepoint of turmeric to the milk just to give the topping a yellow colour. When the bobotie comes out of the oven, pour over the custard. Garnish with the lemon leaves, in a pattern, and return to the oven for a further half hour or until the topping has set. Bobotie is traditionally served with yellow rice and raisins, fruit chutney, sliced ripe bananas and toasted coconut.

YELLOW RICE WITH RAISINS
Serves 6

Yellow rice is known as *begrafnisrys*, or 'funeral rice', in the Cape because it was traditionally served in Malay homes at large family gatherings such as funerals. Rice was either cooked as *droë rys* (dry rice) or *pap rys* (wet rice). This recipe, my variation of a type of pilaff, falls somewhere between the two. Saffron was used in earlier times, but turmeric is the current favourite spice to colour the rice.

You'll need:

340 g basmati rice

125 g seedless raisins

100 g unsalted butter

1 onion, chopped very finely

1 whole peeled clove of garlic

1 piece of stick cinnamon about
  4cm in length

2 cardamom pods, crushed to
  release the seeds

¾ tsp turmeric or some threads
  of saffron

sea salt

freshly milled black pepper

sugar to taste

Method: Place the rice in a bowl and pour over a kettle of boiling water. Stir for a while with a fork and leave to stand for 10 minutes. Pour into a sieve, drain and rinse under cold water. Pour some boiling water over the raisins to plump them up. Melt *half* the butter in a heavy saucepan with a tight-fitting lid. Add the onion and the whole garlic clove and let them sweat gently until the onion is transparent. Add the cinnamon and cardamom pods. Add the rice to the pan, turning it over several times so that each grain is covered in the hot butter. Add the turmeric or saffron, two very good pinches of sea salt and some freshly milled black pepper and 600 ml cold water. Bring quickly to the boil, stirring only a little, and reduce the heat to the lowest level, cover and cook for 11 minutes.

Remove the rice from the heat. Stir in the rest of the butter and gently fork the raisins through the rice as well as about a teaspoon of sugar or more to taste. Cover and leave the rice to stand for 10 minutes. Remove the garlic clove before serving.

Wine suggestion: This is not an easy dish for a wine match. I would suggest that, if the curry is not too strong, an off-dry gewürztraminer from Paul Cluver Wines in Elgin might be a good choice, or a fruity young pinotage, like Ian Starke's Westbridge Pinotage.

MAGGIE PEPLER – Malva Pudding provider to the nation

In the mid-1970s I met Maggie Pepler. She lived in Stellenbosch and had worked for a while at Lanzerac, the country-house hotel. She had also worked in the South African Embassy residences in London and Paris. Maggie is a fabulous cook and to be invited to her home for a meal is an experience that will last me a lifetime – almost 30 years on I can still remember the lamb chops she served with cherries. Food seemed to come out of the tips of her fingers with consummate ease. She has a great and mischievous sense of humour, and things she said in the 1970s still bring a little warm giggle and a smile to my face.

In 1978, Maggie – who had the original recipe for malva pudding – came to work for me at Boschendal Restaurant while our head chef was on holiday. I asked Maggie to teach us how to make this delicious, traditional hot pudding and it has appeared on the buffet at Boschendal Restaurant every day ever since – for more than a quarter of a century. There are many versions of this recipe as people have added a variety of other ingredients, such as banana, apple and even caramelised condensed milk! This is the benchmark Malva Pudding recipe and uses Maggie's original measurements in a 250 ml cup.

ABOVE LEFT: *Maggie in her kitchen at home.*
LEFT: *A rather grander restaurant version of Malva pudding!*

MALVA PUDDING
Serves 6

For the dessert, you'll need:

1 cup flour

1 Tbs bicarbonate of soda

1 cup sugar

1 egg

1 Tbs apricot jam

1 Tbs white vinegar

1 Tbs melted butter

1 cup milk

For the sauce, you'll need:

½ cup cream

½ cup milk

1 cup sugar

½ cup hot water

½ cup butter

Method: Set the oven to 180 °C. Using butter, grease an ovenproof glass or porcelain container approximately 30 cm x 20 cm x 5 cm. Do not use an aluminium, enamel or any metal container. Cut a piece of aluminium foil to cover the dish while the pudding is in the oven and grease it well with butter on one side.

Sift the flour and the bicarb into a bowl and stir in the sugar. In another bowl, beat the egg very well and add the remaining ingredients (excluding those for the sauce) one by one, beating well between each addition. Using a wooden spoon, beat the wet ingredients into the dry ingredients and mix well. Pour the batter into the prepared baking dish, cover with the foil greased-side down and bake for 45 minutes in the preset oven until well risen and brown, and for a further 5 minutes without the foil if not sufficiently brown. If not sufficiently baked, the dessert will not take up all the sauce, making it stodgy inside.

When the pudding is almost done, heat the ingredients for the sauce, ensuring that you melt all the sugar and butter. When the pudding is done, remove it from the oven, take off the foil and pour over the sauce. The pudding will absorb it all. Serve hot, warm or at room temperature, though warm is best, with a little thin cream.

MAGGIE'S STEAMED FRUIT PUDDING
Serves 12 portions

Maggie also made us this really yummy and traditional steamed pudding. This dessert was very popular at Parks Restaurant during the winter. Conveniently for restaurant service, after it has been turned out the pudding can be allowed to get quite cold in the fridge, when it becomes very firm and easy to slice into portions. The portions reconstitute beautifully in the microwave.

You'll need:

185 g sugar

185 ml water

125 ml white vinegar

100 g glacé fruit (50g cherries, 50g fruit)

250 g butter, softened

125 g white sugar

250 g dates, finely chopped

250 g flour

1 tsp bicarbonate of soda

salt

1 egg

1 tsp vanilla essence

250 ml milk

Method: Butter a glass bowl of 2-litre capacity. Have ready a piece of foil, with a fold down the middle, large enough to cover the top, and butter it well. Have ready a piece of muslin and string to tie it over the top of the bowl. Have ready a large pot of water on the boil, with a trivet in it on which to stand the bowl.

Dissolve the sugar in the water and boil for 5 minutes. Add the vinegar and pour this mixture into the base of the bowl. Add the chopped cherries and fruit. Cream the butter well and add the sugar. Beat well for a few minutes. Add the chopped dates and stir them in. Sift the flour, bicarbonate of soda and salt in a separate bowl. Add the egg and vanilla essence to the milk, beat well. Stir the flour mixture and milk mixture alternately into the date mixture. Stir well and pour over the fruit in the bowl. Cover with the prepared foil and muslin, and steam for two hours. Turn out onto a plate with sloping sides to accommodate any sauce that may run down the side of the pudding. Slice and serve with warm vanilla custard.

Wine suggestion: A total cracker of a wine is the Du Toitskloof Hanepoot Jerepigo. My wine writer friend, David Biggs, believes this is one of the finest in the Cape and puts a couple of bottles in the pannier bag of his motorbike whenever he drives past the winery on his way to the Biggs family farm in the Karoo.

MEINERT SYNCHRONICITY

I remember the first time I tasted this wine. We were in the Cellar Room at the wonderful 96 Winery Road Restaurant, eating Natasha Harris's brilliant food. This wine is aptly named, for Martin Meinert has brought together in it the elements of mainly cabernet sauvignon and merlot, with cabernet franc and pinotage, maturing them separately for a year in their French oak barrels and then for a further six months as a blend to synchronise the wines.

Martin's desire to express the terroir of his own farm, Devon Crest in Devon Valley, shows in the perfectly ripe grapes from the southern slopes. The cooler slopes allow for slower ripening and ripe tannins, and the resulting higher sugars give a healthy alcohol count of over 14 %. This wine is more New World in style, with sappy berries and ripe plums performing on an almost savoury vanilla-based oak stage. This wine cries out for food eaten in the company of close friends on a gentle night.

Martin also makes the Ken Forrester Range of wines, among them the FMC – Forrester Meinert Chenin – a wine on the edge of being an icon, which places chenin blanc in the firmament of Cape stars. It is huge and powerful in its fruity flavours, tastes of toasty hazelnut brioche from the spanking new French oak, and is filled out even further – if this is possible – with a splash of 'T' – the Ken Forrester Noble Late Harvest Chenin.

The Gypsy is a romantic Latin swirl of skirts and castanets made from grenache, from one of the few remaining grenache vineyards in Stellenbosch, shiraz and a smidgen of pinotage. She is a warm, charming and appealing wine, tasting of baked plums with sweet spice and hot hedgerow blackberries, and an aroma of cigar box and sweet spices, yet she is serious behind the initial full frontal and very friendly wave. If you are able to bring yourself to leave a bottle or two in the cellar for a while, I am sure the reward would be worth it. But why delay pleasure?

74

CHAPTER NINE

Wine, autumn comfort food and olives

IN EARLY AUTUMN the winelands of the Cape are ahum with activity. The roads between Stellenbosch, Paarl, Franschhoek and Somerset West at any time of the day are plied by more than a few trucks filled with red and white grapes heading for the nearest wine cellar.

For me, the cellars are filled with the smells of my childhood, growing up as I did on a wine farm. That delicious, clean, nose-prickling smell of fermenting must. Of *doppies en stokkies* – the skins and stalks – which have their own unique aroma. I remember large enamel jugs of must being taken into the house to be used by Maggie, our housekeeper, as a raising agent for mosbolletjies, or must buns, which were flavoured with anise and either eaten fresh with bright-yellow farm butter or dried into rusks in the low oven of the Aga in the kitchen and used for early morning teas for weeks afterwards.

What goes on in modern cellars is very different to the more artisanal winemaking practices my father used 50 years ago to make the very acceptable wine we served as a matter of course with meals at home. Visiting Saxenburg Estate, in the Polkadraai Hills outside Stellenbosch, I did a nostalgic cellar-aroma trip, made even more poignant by the sight of concrete tanks with steel doors marked 'Springbok', just like the one in our cellar on Dagbreek. I did notice that the gutters in the floor had been filled in and was reminded of my sister, Helen, aged about four, sitting on her haunches dipping her finger into the must in our gutters and tasting it, with Hector, our brindle boxer, next to her taking the occasional lick too, from her held-out purple finger. He was the first in a series of cellar dogs I have known.

On another occasion I visited Bruce Jack at Flagstone Winery in Somerset West, when the cellar hands were busy punching down the caps of skins into the red wine – an age-old practice. It was heavy, physical work standing on top of the open tank pressing down the skins with a stainless-steel punch that looked as though it was invented by a rocket scientist. And the smells!

For us, harvest time also meant that the chestnuts in our large chestnut orchard would be ripening. We learned soon enough how to prise open the spiky coverings between our shoes so that the ripe, shiny, mahogany nuts would pop out. Back home they were split down the side with a small sharp knife and either boiled or baked in the cool oven of the Aga and eaten hot and floury, burning our fingers and our lips. We also ate them mashed with potato with crumbed and fried joints of the farm chickens, so large that a leg was enough for our vast, little-boy appetites.

Prickly pears are also an autumnal fruit. The huge cactus at the bottom of the garden looked like a series of green plates balanced on top of each other. It was covered in bright-red pears as the days closed in and a nip appeared in the morning air. Maggie had a unique way of picking them. She used an old 'fish tin' that fitted over the pears to snap them off the plant and then laid them in a little pile on the lawn. Using an old broom she swept them slowly up to the front door, by which time all the little thorns had come off. The perfectly ripe pears were put in the fridge and we ate them in ice-cold slices after meals. The overripe ones were cooked up with sugar to make a dark syrup, which was served over thick slices of oven-warm *soetsuurdeeg* (sweet sourdough) bread. The bread, made using a potato to create the leavening, was baked in a huge tin made from a 4-gallon paraffin tin. At the end of the baking, two enormous loaves lay side by side, firm and yeasty. Comfort food indeed.

It was also about this time, as the first chill of autumn caused me to pull up a thin blanket at nighttime, that after some light autumnal rain, white parasol mushrooms would appear on the lawn. They grew in a wide circle and some of them were as large as dinner plates. These were fried in butter and served on toast for supper. In the vineyards, the little brown field mushrooms would cover large areas. These would land up in a mushroom soup or beside a chicken in a red-wine casserole, a Cape version of coq au vin, with a Hermitage or Cinsaut wine replacing the more traditional pinot noir.

Writing of olives in his book *Prospero's Cell,* Lawrence Durrell stated that they had a 'taste older than meat, older than wine. A taste as old as cold water.' On our farm we had an enormous orchard of olive trees – tall, proud, grey trees with long, grey-green leaves. Carefully pruned and tended while young, they stood proud in their soldier-like rows, delivering their wondrous harvest year upon year. The farm is covered with houses now, but several of those trees still stand in gardens all over Durbanville Hills.

And so I grew up being passionate about olives, though I was surprised to learn only the other day that Geoffrey, my brother – who had grown up in identical circumstances – was not an olive person. I think when it comes to olives you either are or are not an olive person. My younger sister, Lilla, when she was aged about four, used to crawl into my bed early in the morning with cold feet and a hand full of olives pinched from a salad in the fridge. She started early. There is a theory that the human being is the only mammal that will return to try foods whose taste it does

not like – olives and beer being among those foods. I have never acquired a taste for beer, but hold me back when it comes to olives.

Those from our orchards were sold to an Italian family in Paarl, who used to come and harvest the fruit themselves. I am not sure whether they used them for oil or for pickling. My mother pickled vast bathfuls of olives using what became known in the family as The First Trumpeter's Method. The First Trumpeter was Roy Lillie, who blew his way through the 1950s and 1960s as first trumpeter in the Cape Town Symphony Orchestra. Outside our kitchen door was a large, white, enamelled bath, one of the ball-and-claw-foot kind which had previously done service in the family bathroom and into which pots and pans and plates were now dumped during family parties in the pre-dishwasher days. It also did sterling service during the olive season.

Olive picking was a family occasion of great fun. Hessian was spread out under the trees and Geoff and I were deputed to get up into the trees and shake them furiously to make the fruit come raining down. We also used long-handled rakes to retrieve them. We had a very eccentric aunt, who decided in her very bohemian, flowing-scarves way that upside-down umbrellas were the real

Olives add colour to a salad, their oil the best dressing with black pepper, sea salt, a dash of verjuice and a spoonful of mustard.

way to catch the olives. 'It prevents them from being bruised, dear.' But The First Trumpeter's Method required that the olives be gently crushed before being cured, so bruised olives really didn't matter. Fortunately, bohemian aunt got tired fairly soon after running round the tree trying to catch the olives in Grandfather's large, black, London-bought, Fox Frame umbrella.

The olives were poured into the bath and the curing process began, to remove the extremely bitter substance oleuropein, named for the tree's botanical name, *Olea europaea*. The presence of oleuropein prevents olives being eaten fresh off the tree, so that part of the farm was not as well protected as the vineyards were! The bulk of our olives were water-cured and a small amount was cured with brine. Water-curing involved submerging the olives in water and changing the water each day, until the bitterness was no longer present. Brine was changed every two weeks. When the olives were pronounced ready, they were bottled in a brine solution or in olive oil and herbs, and put away in the dark, cool corners of the wine cellar to 'pickle' for a couple of months before being ready for consumption.

We should wonder at man's resourcefulness to transform this bitter little fruit into something deliciously edible and into the most sublime of oils for cooking. Certainly South Africans tend to be like northern Europeans, in that we have a butter culture, but the swing to olive oil is taking place and there are olive orchards being planted all over the Cape. I am told there is a thriving olive business in Namibia, though climatically olives prefer growing near the sea, in a Mediterranean climate, where there are long hot summers and sufficiently low temperatures in winter to allow for the setting of the fruit.

Some of our olive-oil manufacturers are doing fabulously well in terms of quality. Morgenster is among them, bearding the lion in its den and snatching trophies from under the noses of Italian producers. One of our favourites is Kloovenburg, and Maradadi, made by Mike Smith from Worcester. And then there are the almost household names of Costa and Vesuvio, which are more generally available in most South African food stores.

The superchefs of television food channels and coffee-table cookbooks slosh olive oil about everywhere, into their Teflon-lined pans, onto their designer-leaf salads, into their mayos and aiolis, salad dressings and pestos, over roasted heads of garlic and vegetables and, yes, even into an Olive Oil and Sauternes cake courtesy of Chez Panisse in the Californian winelands. Can one use such a generous, historical, mythical, magical oil with circumspection? I think not.

PETER VADAS'S STEAMED GOLDEN SYRUP PUDDING
Serves 6

This is real autumn comfort food. Peter and Vivienne Vadas own Pembreys Restaurant at Belvidere Estate in Knysna, where we eat often and very happily. Their son PJ worked for us at Parks Restaurant and went on to London to carve out a career with Gordon Ramsay in London. How lucky we are to have this sort of talent and passion among our young people and how well we will eat when he returns to home shores.

You'll need:

125 ml golden syrup

2 extra large eggs

180 g white sugar

sea salt

½ tsp vanilla essence

250 g soft butter

125 g self-raising flour

45 ml milk

Method: With extra butter, grease well a 2-litre pudding bowl and place a round of buttered greaseproof paper at the base. I have also used very successfully a glass, loaf-shaped dish – makes the pudding easier to cut into slices if you're serving it in a restaurant. Pour half the golden syrup into the bowl and set aside. Place the remaining ingredients into a food processor and pulse till well blended. Tip the batter over the syrup in the base of the prepared pudding bowl. Seal for steaming with a sheet of buttered greaseproof paper and a layer of foil. Both sheets should have a good fold in the middle. Tie a piece of string round the foil.

Place the bowl on a trivet in a pot containing just-boiling water, enough to come about two thirds of the way up the bowl. Lower the heat until the water just shudders and steam for two hours. Make sure the pot does not boil dry; add boiling water to keep it well filled. When done, allow to cool for a short while to firm up, turn out the pudding onto a hot plate and pour over the remaining syrup which has been heated in a microwave. Serve with very thick, cold cream.

Wine suggestion: Van der Hum, the liqueur made from naartjies, a soft, easy-peeling tangerine. This classic Cape liqueur was similar to citrus liqueurs made in the West Indies and, according to C Louis Leipoldt, 'probably also in China'. It is made with brandy, flavoured with naartjie peel and an array of spices – cinnamon, cloves, nutmeg and mace. Can't get more traditional than this.

GIORGIO DALLA CIA – Wild mushrooms, wild Italians and grappa

When my brother Geoff and I were little boys, our parents knew Miss E L Stevens who was *the* mushroom fundi of the Cape – we were in awe of her. On Sundays, the stoep of her little cottage in Rosebank was lined with baskets of fungi brought from the forests near the city by enthusiastic mushroom-hunters wanting her to identify them as edible. Sometimes, there would be a poisonous one in the basket and she would make the picker throw them all away. She had no fatalities that we ever heard of!

In May, the mountains of the Cape are filled with Italians (and other mad fungus-lovers) looking for wild mushrooms. Be they cèpes (aka porcini or penny buns), pine rings or big, open, field mushrooms, they all land up firstly in wicker baskets and then in tummies.

One of the best times I've had was picking mushrooms with a fungi-maniac of note, Giorgio dalla Cia. One of the great elder-statesman wine-makers of the Cape, his job description, at its most basic, is Winemaker and Distiller. But it's like calling Michelangelo a sculptor or Picasso a painter. Behind the person there is just so much more. Don't ever ask him where he picks his porcini and pine rings. He comes over all vague and

Giorgio and his son George.

you get general descriptions like 'in the mountains near Stellenbosch'. Accurate in his locations he is not. If people stop in the forest to admire our full baskets and dare to ask 'Where?', they are as likely to be sent off on a wild goose chase over the top of the closest and highest mountain peak.

He would kill me if I told you where we went picking, so I shan't, and what an amazing experience it was. Instructions as to the meeting point were precise, and as for the time it was 'Be there at 07h 30'. In my wildest dreams I was not going to be late. I was also given very strict instructions on what to wear – hat, because you crawl through the bush; thick trousers, because you crawl through the bush; and boots, because you crawl through the bush; a wicker basket in which to place your pickings; and a long-bladed knife with which to release the little treasures from the earth.

Giorgio is totally overcome in nature. 'Isn't the silence of the forest just majestic? It's like speaking to God!' 'I find my ancestral feelings to feed myself coming back while walking on the carpet of needles.' And he is careful to spread the spores widely so that there will be more for next

80

year. We picked bright-orange, lactating pine rings which he told us his wife, Simonetta, cooks in a cream sauce and serves with pasta. Over-ripe and slimy mushrooms were picked too. And he taught us to cut the little piggy (porcini) stumps like chips and fry them in olive oil, and to dry what we didn't immediately use for later use in sauces, soups and casseroles as flavour-enhancers. Who needs MSG? And ever since, I have been prepared to do almost anything to eat fresh wild mushrooms.

Having retired from Meerlust Estate, Giorgio has a new job – distilling grappa and making two, delicious, own-label Dalla Cia wines, a sauvignon blanc and a chardonnay. His son George markets the products, which include some sinful grappa chocolates (shells of dark chocolate which explode grappa into your mouth), and a seriously delicious pair of vanilla and chocolate grappa ice-creams. After mushrooming with Giorgio on chill autumn mornings we are always warmed with little nips of his grappa.

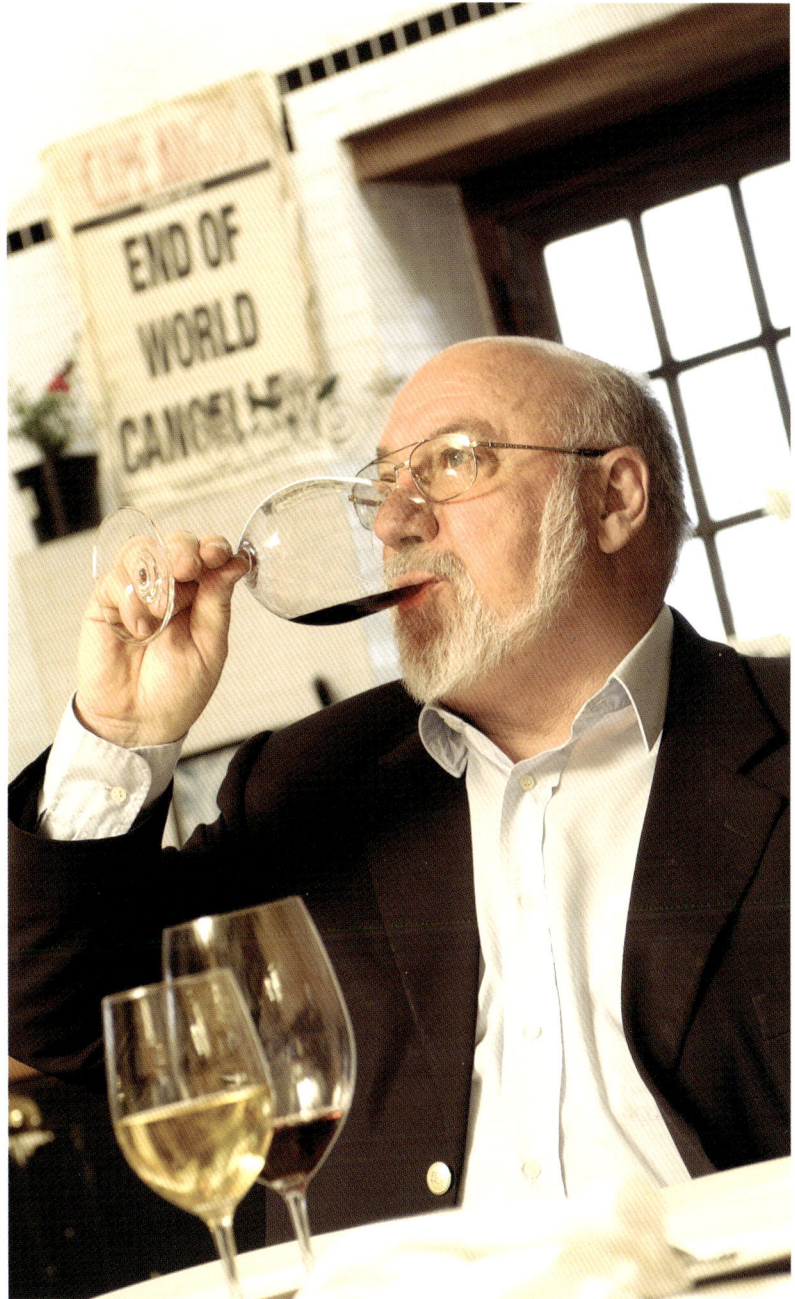

Giorgio dalla Cia - one of my favourite people.

RISOTTO FOR GIORGIO
Serves 6

You'll need:

10 g dried porcini, chopped

50 g butter

olive oil

1 medium onion, chopped

125 g streaky bacon, chopped
   fairly fine

2 sticks celery, chopped fairly fine

2 medium carrots, chopped fairly fine

4 cloves garlic, chopped fairly fine

4 sprigs young rosemary, chopped
   fairly fine

2 large sprigs flat-leafed parsley
   with stems, chopped fairly fine

2 large sprigs marjoram, chopped
   fairly fine

340 g arborio rice

250 ml good red wine

125 g baby button mushrooms,
   quartered

250 g portobellini (chestnut)
   mushrooms, sliced

250 g medium-sized, open, brown
   mushrooms, roughly chopped

1 litre boiling vegetable or
   chicken stock

1 x 410 g tin red kidney beans,
   drained

salt and freshly ground black pepper

Method: Place the porcini in a small bowl and cover with boiling water to swell. The soaking water will be added later to the risotto. In a heavy-bottomed casserole, heat the butter in the olive oil and add the onion. Cook slowly until just turning golden, add the bacon and cook a while till the fat has been released and is browning gently. Add the celery, carrots, garlic and herbs. Stir-fry for a while till the vegetables are soft. Add the rice and stir while it heats up and each kernel is well covered in oil. Add the wine and cook a while. Add the mushrooms and then add the stock, slowly stirring all the while. Stirring is very important because it stops the risotto from sticking to the base of the pot and it helps with the emulsification of the sauces with the starch from the rice. When all the stock is added, the rice should be cooked. Test it, and if it is still a bit hard, add a bit of boiling water and stir a while longer. Add the beans and heat through. Season really well. Stir in a couple of large lumps of butter and allow to stand for about 10 minutes or so. Eat with generous sprinklings of freshly grated Grana Padana or Parmigiana-Reggiano. The addition of a couple of slices of salami, chopped, at the time of adding the bacon, will add another flavour to the mix.

Wine suggestion: It must be one of Giorgio's, perhaps the Meerlust Pinot Noir or the Dalla Cia Chardonnay.

THE DALLA CIA WINES

Giorgio dalla Cia came to notice early in his career as the winemaker of the top-marque wine estate, Meerlust, in Stellenbosch. Here, and first with Nico and latterly with Hannes Myburgh, he produced world-class reds and a superb chardonnay, until his retirement in early 2004.

I am particularly fond of the Dalla Cia Sauvignon Blanc which is made in an overtly Sancerre style rather than the flashily upfront and fruity New World style. I find this a wonderfully minerally wine with a bracing flavour of sea foam and kelp – fresh and green.

The Dalla Cia Chardonnay is untrammelled by oak, leaving the clear citrus to sing surrounded by a chorus of the other more characteristic chardonnay flavours. There is a breadth of flavour in this wine that makes it very much a food wine to accompany the Italian dishes so loved by this family.

Watch out for the first Bordeaux-style red blend from this foremost of the Cape winemakers, a gentle giant of a man.

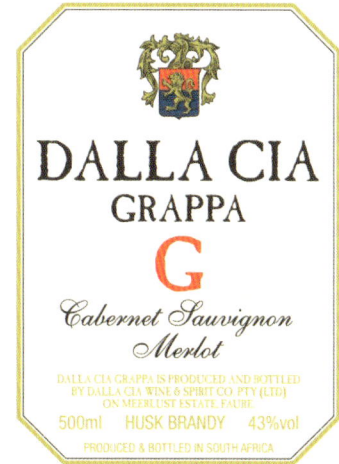

*The cep or edible Boletus (*Boletus edulis*), Steinpilz in German, pennybun in English and steenswam in Afrikaans.*

83

CHAPTER TEN

Wayside Food

ETERNITY IN OUR FAMILY WOULD HAVE BEEN VERY SHORT if we had applied the definition of it famously described by American writer and critic, Dorothy Parker, as 'two people and a ham'.

You see, when I was a child (the 1950s, since you ask), we were great picnickers. We were wayside eaters and beach lunchers, big time. Leftover ham and other foods were used up fast. Not for us the plastic food of the new-millennium, petrol-station eateries plonked one hour apart on the national highways.

We had a picnic basket, a great big brute of a rattan-and-wire thing made by the Civilian Blind in Salt River, which served a double purpose when we took our cat to the vet in the village. It needed two people to carry it but fitted into the boot of our avocado-green, 1948 Studebaker in which we bumped about the Cape for most of my childhood, tossing sweets and pennies at the farm children who opened gates for us. And there was just enough room left in the boot for bathers and towels if we happened to come across a dam or cool clear mountain stream somewhere. Being a family of twitchers, the binoculars and *Roberts' Birds of Southern Africa* came too. There were also blankets, which were called 'leatherins', and a motley array of jerseys and sun hats and bottles of the evil-smelling, brown suntan oil with which we were liberally and reluctantly smeared should the sun dare peek its head out from behind the clouds. The wine and drinks were wrapped with ice in old beach towels.

The basket was lined with a fringed, white, seersucker tablecloth which, when opened, revealed a magical array of treasures from our farm kitchen, usually wrapped up in greaseproof paper, tied with cotton and marked with pencil or packed in waxed boxes. It was from this basket that, as a child, I ate foods one reads about in articles by Elizabeth David and Margaret Costa. My aunt Marge, who lived in Gumtree in the Free State, kept geese. When they were slaughtered, she kept the livers and made what she called 'lean' pâté de foie gras. It was served on crustless white bread thinly spread with yellow Gumtree butter, and I can taste it still.

There were sandwiches containing cucumber – not today's burp-free English cucumbers, but short, stubby, green thumbs with hard pips in the middle. They had the cap cut off and then were rubbed on the cut end 'to remove the bitterness' and sliced down the middle. The pips were removed and then the cucumber halves were sliced thinly, salted and drained in a blue enamel colander. Watercress grew in the streams on the farm and added such pepperiness to the sand-wiches. These were often made with 'boermeel' bread, which was not quite brown meal, and which had been 'started' with a potato ferment or some grape must taken from one of the open concrete tanks in the cellar. There were fat egg-mayo sandwiches flavoured with chopped chives, sandwiches filled with Miss Grace Baxter's potted meat (made from her leftover ham and a veal knuckle), and cape gooseberry turnovers made with Mrs Norton's puff pastry ('I always use a bottle of sparkling Van Riebeeck water, my dear, it makes the pastry much lighter.'). There was Mrs Roberts's mebos – made from dried apricots. These fat, orange roundels of tart sappy fruit were coated in crunchy, Jamaican demerara sugar, now available again in the shops, post-liberation. (We first met Mrs Roberts by accident in Hermanus and she invited us in to tea and served her mebos.) And wrapped in a damp cloth there was also an Olivier version of poundcake. Our picnics weren't complete without rooibos tea, rich red pools of it poured from enormous Thermos flasks that looked like military surplus.

School lunches could also be regarded as wayside food in a way. Amy and Peter's lunch boxes were legendary at school. Where other kids would have a scrawny apricot jam sandwich, Amy would take a lunch box almost the same size as her school bag filled with Coronation Chicken with seedless grapes and other boxes filled with slices of salami, biltong, peeled ripe mango, let-tuce salad with pitted olives, feta and carrot strips and small boxes of fruit juice frozen overnight so that she would have cold drinks at breaktime. Peter's favourites are white rolls with roast chick-en mayonnaise or thickly spread with Nutella chocolate spread and a tub of black seedless grapes!

THE ULTIMATE CHEESE AND TOMATO SANDWICH
Serves 1

You will not find a coffee shop or snack bar in South Africa that does not serve a cheese and tomato sandwich. There are minimum requirements for my ultimate cheese and tomato sandwich. Fry some finely chopped onion slowly in butter until caramelised and cool it to room temperature on kitchen paper. Have ready an excellent bread knife – it'll do for both the bread and the tomato. You'll need fresh, soft, white bread, preferably home-made and containing bread flour rather than cake flour, and made in a large loaf tin, which will give you a large sandwich! Good tomatoes are important, vine-ripened in the sun to the point of perfection, plump and firm for easy slicing. The cheese? My choice would be Gay van Hasselt's Prince Albert Royal, coarsely grated. This is an unpasteurised cheese and is best described as a Farm Gouda, though it has flavour elements of a mild cheddar – you want the taste of the tomato to shine through.

You'll need:

1 onion, finely chopped
unsalted butter
2 slices white bread, homebaked
by preference
1 perfectly ripe tomato,
    preferably vine-ripened
sea salt
freshly milled black pepper
fresh Sweet Basil leaves
grated cheese - Prince Albert
    Royal is my favourite
handful of rocket leaves
verjuice
olive oil

For the construction: Cut two slices of bread in medium to thick slices and spread with soft unsalted butter. Thinly spread over some onion. Slice the tomato thinly and layer it generously over the onion, season well with my favourite Velddrif, hand-harvested sea salt and freshly milled black pepper. Top with torn, sweet-basil leaves, pile on the grated cheese and top with the other slice of bread. Slice the sandwich on the diagonal and serve with rocket dressed with verjuice and olive oil of the extra virgin kind. Wrapped up, the flavours will meld in the waiting for it to be consumed.

Wine suggestion: If you're making this to eat at home, all through the making thereof and its consumption you need to be drinking a chilled pinot noir from the Bouchard Finlayson vineyards, a grenache/shiraz blend from Ken Forrester Wines or a luscious, fat chardonnay – Jordan Nine Yards would do well. A treat we make on occasion when we have a barbecue is to put the sandwich together and tie it in a little parcel with some sewing cotton, and when the coals are cooling, lightly toast the sandwich on both sides. This will cause the cheese to melt slightly and ooze out of the sides. Yum!

AMY AND PETER'S FAVOURITE CHOC CHIP COOKIES

Makes 24 large biscuits or 48 smaller ones. I recommend 25 g raw mixture for a good size.

For a more modern wayside eatable, here is a 1990s recipe used by a chef I knew who used to go round Cape Town selling goodies to office blocks. We used to buy these Choc Chip Cookies from her and my children just loved them.

You'll need:

90 g butter

90 g white sugar

90 g brown sugar

5 ml vanilla essence

1 egg

180 g self-raising flour

1 ml salt

60 g chopped pecans

120 g chopped dark chocolate

Method: Pre-heat oven to 180 °C. Grease two baking trays lightly with sunflower oil. Cream the butter with the sugars and the vanilla essence. Beat the egg and add to the mixture with a spoonful of flour to prevent curdling. Sift the flour and salt together twice and beat into the mixture. Add the nuts and chopped chocolate. Spoon the mixture onto greased baking sheets. Bake for 12-15 minutes. Place on a cooling rack.

Back, left to right: Maddy, Peter, Amy, Roland Heidemann who lives with us because Trixie his mother works in England, and Geoff. Front, left to right: Lilla with her enchanting boys Oliver and Dylan, me and Sarah my daughter.

NO ORDINARY CARROT CAKE

Serves 8-10 generous slices.

Every coffee-and-cake shop will offer you a Carrot Cake, usually with a runny cream-cheese icing. None of the recipes I have seen have really appealed to me because most of them have oil in the recipe and I wanted to add the flavour of butter. My children like this one – I always view them as my best critics.

You'll need:

180 g flour

1 tsp each bicarbonate of soda
   and baking powder

½ tsp mixed spices (or some
   grated dried root ginger and
   nutmeg)

¼ tsp salt

180 g butter

180 g sugar

2 whole eggs, lightly beaten

½ tsp vanilla essence

400 ml grated carrots

50 g chopped skinned almonds

125 ml chopped pineapple

75 ml roasted sesame seeds

Method: Prepare a 1.5 litre loaf tin. Begin by buttering the base well. Cut a piece of greaseproof paper the size of the base, insert it into the loaf tin and sprinkle lightly with some sesame seeds and then flour. Set the oven to 180 °C. Have ready a cake rack to cool the cake on after it comes out of the oven.

Sieve together the flour, bicarbonate of soda, baking powder, spices and salt, twice. In the bowl of a food processor, cream the butter and then add the sugar in a stream and whisk it till light and fluffy. Add the eggs, one at a time, adding a heaped spoonful of the flour mixture with each egg to prevent curdling. Add the vanilla essence. Turn into a bowl. Add the remaining flour and beat well with a wooden spoon. Add the carrots, almonds, pineapple and sesame seeds, and beat well. Turn into the prepared loaf tin and smooth over the top.

Bake in the preset oven for about 45 minutes or until a skewer inserted into the centre comes out clean. Remove from the oven, place the tin on the cake rack and allow to cool in the tin for at least 15 minutes. Remove from the tin and invert on the cake rack, cover with a colander and allow to cool completely and for the outside of the cake to dry off. Coat the top of the cake with your favourite cream cheese or lemon icing and garnish with toasted almonds.

HANNES MYBURGH – custodian of Meerlust

Hannes and his parents came into my life in the late 1960s when I worked at Lanzerac, and on family occasions they lunched or dined at Lanzerac.

Today, Hannes inhabits Meerlust, which must surely be one of the most spectacular of the early manor houses that dot the Cape winelands. The house itself is a perfect piece of Cape Dutch architecture, with the most impressive array of dwellings and farm buildings, gardens and trees. It is spectacular, too, because of its setting, with its west-facing front door looking directly onto Table Mountain and to the east the Helderberg. Hannes, with becoming humility, knows his place in the history of this farm, which is interwoven in the social fabric of early and current life in the Cape.

Important people have stayed at and visited Meerlust. The less important, too, have come away with the sense of comfort and wellbeing in which the spirit of Meerlust envelops them.

A mutual friend, Phillida Brooke Simons, wrote a book called *Meerlust: 300 Years of Hospitality*, which tells the story of Meerlust from the time the land was granted to Henning Huising in July 1693 to the present day. No dry, dusty, history book this – it reads so easily and held me enthralled at the comings and goings at Meerlust, almost as if I was watching a movie in which I had a minor part. Hannes invited me to provide a recipe for the book – a great honour for me to be there and in the company of some of the top chefs of the Cape.

To sit at the huge square table in the kitchen and enjoy Meerlust cook Bettie Brown's Waterblommetjiebredie with creamy baked pumpkin and eat her crusty white bread is the closest to culinary heaven you will ever get. And years later I am still trying to get the pumpkin recipe out of her!

Hannes dined at Parks Restaurant on a couple of occasions – his bold signature and message of love in our visitors' book is something I treasure.

Hannes Myburgh, custodian of Meerlust, he of the beautiful eyes and kind, gentle, loving spirit.

ORANGE AND VAN DER HUM CRÈME BRÛLÉE FOR HANNES
Serves 4

Quintessential to the Cape is Van der Hum, a liqueur made from tangerines by many old Cape families.

You'll need:

3 egg yolks

½ Tbs sugar

300 ml double cream

1 vanilla pod or 1 tsp vanilla
   extract

75 ml orange juice, reduced from
   150 ml

45 ml Van der Hum

Method: Have ready four, small, earthenware ramekins. Mix the egg yolks with the sugar. Heat the cream and the vanilla pod or extract in a saucepan until just about to boil and pour over the eggs, whisking all the while. Add the orange juice and Van der Hum. Return to the saucepan and to medium heat and cook, stirring until the mixture coats the back of a wooden spoon. Do not allow the mixture to boil. Strain out the vanilla pod if used. Pour the mixture into the moulds, cover with plastic wrap and chill overnight. Next day, sprinkle over some castor sugar and caramelise with a blowtorch. Serve with sablé biscuits flavoured with Van der Hum.

Wine suggestion: Van der Hum or Mandarine Napoleon – a mandarin liqueur.

*Meerlust, one of the most
beautiful manor houses in
the winelands.*

SPRINGFIELD ESTATE WHOLE BERRY CABERNET

I am amused by the names given to some wines by winemakers in the Cape – Swahili words and Italian names are totally inappropriate in my view. Then along comes the sibling team of Abrie and Jeannette Bruwer, of Springfield Estate in Robertson, with names so carefully chosen that you simply have to taste the wines immediately, if not sooner.

Life from Stone is the moniker of one of their sauvignon blancs. The very name conjures up the flintstone and freshly exploded gunpowder detectable in the nose. The delicious aromas and taste of pears are coun-

tered by a bracing acidity. Their Special Cuvée is a sauvignon blanc with a more meaty body. And there is the Méthode Ancienne Cabernet Sauvignon that uses only the native yeasts from its own vineyard. It's a similar story for the Wild Yeast Chardonnay.

The Cape's most urbane wine merchant, John Collins, who has a fine collection of wines in his briefcase, introduced us to the Springfield Estate Whole Berry Cabernet. This wine is now a permanent feature in our house, enjoyed hugely by Maddy and me and our daughter Amy.

Abrie uses the natural vineyard yeasts for fermentation and gently extracts full flavour and gentle ripe tannins from whole bunches of uncrushed grapes. It is boldly blackcurrant and brushed with excellent oak which adds hints of vanilla and creamy dark chocolate melted in mocha as a background for the lusciousness and sappiness of the other dark fruit and ripe plums.

A couple of years ago, Abrie put a wire cage of red wine on the ocean floor on the southern coast. He lost it for a while and then found it and took it back to the farm. It will be interesting to see what effect the gently rolling, cold South Atlantic Ocean will have on the wine. And what will he call it? Like Sebastian the lobster in *The Little Mermaid*, Under the Sea?

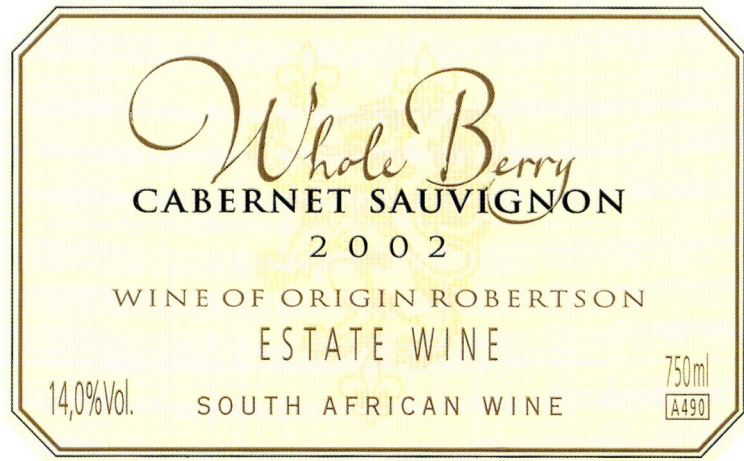

91

CHAPTER ELEVEN

Lanzerac – my grand old lady

IN THE SUMMER OF 1966, I was working at the Riviera Hotel in Hermanus, then owned by the Morgan-Edwards family, who were West Country hoteliers from England. The hotel was open for the summer only and a great family trek took place twice a year across the equator. There are things I was taught there that today, even in the computer-oriented world of reservations and notekeeping, stand me in good stead. And the fountain of this knowledge was Elsie Morgan-Edwards. I can still picture her with her head cocked to the side, to prevent the smoke rising from the cigarette dangling from her lips from going into her eye. 'This is your bible, my boy,' she would say, patting the huge reservations charts that looked as if they kept pencil- and eraser-makers operating at high profit.

There were some incredible characters working there – Mr Keller, the asthmatic elderly chef who had been a chef at Glyndebourne for 30 years; Martin Pike, his assistant, who used to make the classical confections for the dessert trolley; and Joycie, his wife, who reigned supreme in the housekeeping room behind her sewing machine. The food was the classic Grand Hotel variety, with hors d'oeuvres and dessert trolleys, French sauces and steamed puddings, duckling à l'orange and grilled lamb cutlets financière, and a wine list featuring many imported wines.

Some of the most exotic characters would visit the Riviera. Tiny and Stuart Cloete would appear for the Saturday-night, black-tie dinner dance – he, the famous South African writer, statuesque and a superb dancer; she, petite with a bird-like American-accented voice. There was a Mrs Beattie, with whom nearly all the guests used to lunch during their stay. The Chief Justice of St Helena, Evan Wyndham, and his Scottish wife, Johnny, were regulars too and poured many a gin and tonic by their poolside for British visitors. Peter Allen's eponymous grocery store was certainly able to replace for visitors most of what Fortnum & Mason and Harrods could provide, and delivered bowls of fruit and sweets to their hotel rooms at the Bay View, the Marine, the Birkenhead and the Riviera hotels.

After the family sold the Riviera, and the hotel was about to close down for the winter, I needed a job, so I applied to Lanzerac because I had been told that this was 'the' place to go and work to further my career.

I made an appointment with the owner, David Rawdon, and went off to meet him. He appeared in the sitting room with an apron on and the back of his hand covered in chocolate mousse. As I got to know him better in the following years, I knew that he had put the mousse there specially so that I would get it on my hand! I worked there as an apprentice for nearly three years, for R60.00 a month, today the price of three of the most basic dishes McDonald's of the golden arches has on offer.

Thus started three years of the most fascinating time of my life – which led to three more in the mid-1970s, when I went back there as Manager. And it was there that I was to employ Maddy, and then marry her.

David Rawdon, now in his 80s, is one of the most hardworking people I have ever met. He instilled into me so much of what I am aware of as a person today – and he probably does not even know it: the way chairs are set out on either side of a window or door, the length of a table-cloth, how one arranges furniture, flowers, food on a plate, etc, etc, etc. He is a superb interior decorator and designer with an instinctive touch for a warm and comfortable and friendly feel. And could he party! The one thing that always amazed me was that he could go to bed, no matter how early in the morning, no matter how huge the party and yet he was always in the kitchen at 7 in the morning. He might not have been saying much or able to see properly, but he would sit there drinking cup upon cup of boiling water watching breakfast being set up. He was punctual, almost painfully so.

Lanzerac was a lovely country-house hotel, chosen even in those days as one of the top 300 hotels of the world in a guidebook by René le Claire of *Harpers & Queen*. There were very few, if any, country-house hotels in South Africa in those days and certainly the b&b business had not even started. Each one of the hotel's bedrooms was individually decorated, former stables and hen houses among them, with lovely imported fabrics and lots of antique furniture, for which David had an uncanny eye and of which he had a large collection.

Lanzerac was also very well known for its Sunday night buffet supper, which was booked out three months in advance, and its cheese lunch, with a glass of wine and a bowl of soup, 20 cheeses, and home-made brown bread all for 95c, which today would not even buy a newspaper. There was also a lunch in the cellar bar, in the cellar under the manor house. Breakfast was a grand affair in the English style, from freshly squeezed orange and grapefruit juices, all the cereals, toast and preserves, to kippers, eggs of every description, beef and pork sausages, and kidneys and mushrooms. Quite often, ladies would have breakfast sent up to their room and their husbands would come into the dining room for breakfast and read the papers. One Ghurka Colonel refused to talk until after breakfast – head-nodding was all he wanted to do before his kipper. Certain of the widowed guests came in to breakfast and would 'hold court' on the patio outside afterwards. One of my favourites, Lady Southby – Iris to us all – who kept coming to Lanzerac till she was in her 90s, always chose a table with at least six chairs at it where the troops would gather after they finished breakfast, to smoke and chat.

Lanzerac, still holds a special place in my heart. It was here that I met Maddy, employed her, then married her.

There were the amusing eccentrics, like a large, white-haired, mutton-chopped Scottish chap who used to announce his arrival at reception thus: 'My name is Hamilton and I come from the Kingdom of Fife!' Mr and Mrs Wyman Abbott, a very elderly couple from Peterborough, came

94

each year. She wore a pair of real kid gloves and smoothed a real linen cloth onto her lap each morning to read the newspaper. When she had finished, her husband would wash them and hang them out to dry over the back of the chairs outside their room. There was Captain Maude who was a tiny little man, immaculately dressed in the most perfect clothes and who walked with two walking sticks. He brought Ian Smith (then Prime Minister of Rhodesia) and his wife, Janet, and Clifford Dupont (first President of Rhodesia) and his wife, Armenell, to stay. Hughie, who lived in Ireland, became a great friend and when I was a cookery student in London he took me to dinner at The Connaught, where he always stayed. At the Lanzerac, he used to sit all day in a chair underneath the oaks on the back lawn. There were usually a couple of chairs there and people would 'pop in' on him. He was slightly secretive about what he did and would mutter *sotto voce* about bearing messages from Lord So-and-So to 'the Rhodesians'. He was known as The Oracle on account of being consulted by all.

Lanzerac is outside the pretty university town of Stellenbosch. The town is still small, surrounded by farms that mainly produce the fine wines for which the area is well known. In the late 1960s, Stellenbosch University was a whites-only, Afrikaans-language university and a hotbed of the Nationalist Party and the Dutch Reformed Church. It usually had a Prime Minister or some noteworthy of the previous regime as Chancellor. On the day that Hendrik Verwoerd was assassinated in Parliament, I saw respected citizens of the town, businessmen and lawyers weeping in the streets.

Each year, many British visitors would stay at Lanzerac – we called them 'the swallows'. Some would come for a short stay and others would come for up to three months. In the late 1960s, most of them would travel out on the Ellerman & Bucknall Line boats, usually called something like *City of Exeter,* and some would travel on the Union Castle boats, which were normally named for famous British castles, like *Windsor Castle.* The passengers would disembark at Cape Town and be taken up to the Mount Nelson Hotel, the Victorian pink palace at the top of The Company Gardens, where they would spend a couple of weeks to acclimatise. The hotel transport would meet them off the gangplank, and Louis – the large, Wagnerian, bass-voiced, Swiss concierge (who was succeeded by his son Richard) – would meet them on arrival, remember them well and make sure they were in the same room as the previous year. Eric the waiter would look after them and, sure as anything, dear old Judy would still be the chambermaid. They would all bow and scrape and smile and happily accept the tips so generously handed out by these kind Britons. And because they presented this ever-smiling face, many of the swallows used to think that the 'serving classes' were such happy people and that all was well with the world. How wrong they were.

After a bit of acclimatisation at the 'Nellie', they would venture forth from Cape Town, usually to Hermanus. They would be fetched in large American sedans by Tommy McClelland or her partner, who was known only as Mrs Kostick. Tommy had been General Smuts's driver during the Second World War, and until the 1990s people in Hermanus used her to take them to Cape Town, 'because, you know, she's such a wonderful driver and can take a car to pieces and fix it if it breaks down'.

Others would go to Lanzerac for the full time. An elderly chinchilla breeder from Midhurst, Sussex, used to bring her Daimler on the boat, offload at dawn in Cape Town harbour and arrive at Lanzerac for lunch. She continued to come for many years.

A number of visitors disembarked in Cape Town while the boats went up the coast to Durban, stayed at the 'Nellie' or the President, and then got back on the boats and went home. This gave them a good 5-6 weeks away from home at the coldest time of the year.

I met a diversity of people at Lanzerac: Dame Edith Evans, Zena Dare, Stephane Grappelli the jazz violinist, Narciso Yepes the Spanish guitarist, Robert and Ethel Kennedy, Jean Shrimpton, Major-General Sir Francis (Freddie) de Guingand who was on Montgomery's staff during World War 2, Lord King who was the chairman of British Airways, and many academics from abroad who came to work at the university – one a wine man called Cornelius Ough, who stayed for months on end with his wife and daughter.

One couple, who became my surrogate grandparents, were Colonel and Mrs J C E Harding Rolls, or Uncle Jack and Aunt Eve. He was the nephew of Charles Rolls, the partner of Henry Royce; together they built the first Rolls Royce. When I went to live in England in 1968, I spent a lot of time with them in their home in Monmouth.

Today, Lanzerac is owned by Christo Wiese, a Cape Town entrepreneur who as a student consumed many a glass on the oak-shaded veranda outside the bar at Lanzerac. It has its own winery again, taking up a tradition for top-quality wine which had ended after Angus Buchanan's last vintage in 1959. The hotel is not the gentle, laid-back country house it was when I first started working there in 1966. It is architecturally still the same, being a national monument, but it is professionally run as an excellent modern hotel should be.

MOCHA MOUSSE FOR DAVID
Serves 6

This was not the mousse spread over the back of David's hand when I first met him back in the 1960s. I don't recall even seeing chocolate with 70% cocoa butter then. You really need excellent chocolate for a mousse like this, so don't skimp on the dark stuff.

You'll need:
200 g dark chocolate
2 Tbs coffee liqueur like Kahlua
4 eggs, separated
2 Tbs good brandy or Grand
    Marnier
125 g castor sugar
200 g unsalted butter, cut into
    tiny blocks
pinch fine salt
a squeeze of lemon juice or a drop
    of wine vinegar

Method: Melt the chocolate in a glass bowl set over barely simmering water in a saucepan. Once all melted, stir in the coffee liqueur and take the bowl off the saucepan. Place the egg yolks in another bowl, together with a tablespoon of water and the brandy or Grand Marnier. Remove a tablespoon of the sugar and add the remaining sugar to the egg mixture. Place over the saucepan of simmering water, and using an eggbeater, beat steadily until the mixture becomes thick, white and fluffy. Remove from the heat and beat for a while while cooling. Place the bowl containing the chocolate on the saucepan again and whisk the butter into the chocolate. Take it off the heat and fold it gently but thoroughly into the egg yolk mixture, using the edge of a metal spoon. In another large clean bowl place the egg whites and strew over a pinch of salt and a squeeze of lemon or a tiny splash of wine vinegar, and whisk with an electric beater until it reaches the soft peak stage. Then add the reserved castor sugar and beat until stiff. Using the metal spoon, fold in a good spoonful of the meringue into the chocolate and egg mixture to soften it. Then carefully, again using the edge of a metal spoon, fold the meringue into the chocolate mixture. Pour into a fine glass or crystal bowl and refrigerate for at least 5 hours. Garnish with finely grated chocolate and serve with whipped cream flavoured with some instant espresso coffee and sugar.

Wine suggestion: Engeltjipipi – 'angel's wee' – a lipsmacking, botrytised semillon-based blend with some tangerine overtones, from Nicky and Mary Krone's Twee Jonge Gezellen Estate in Tulbagh. Actually, come to think of it, their Rosé Brut bubbly would be fun to go with this too, nice and palate-cleansing!

JOS BAKER – Living National Treasure

I first met Jos Baker at Eagle's Nest, where she and her photographer husband, David, lived in the winelands of Constantia. I took my small daughter, Sarah, there in the early 1970s to watch fire flies in the forest.

Jos was then the editor of a fashion magazine, which if memory serves me correctly was called *The Buyer*. Now a freelance journalist, Jos edits *Wine* magazine's guide, *Top 100 Restaurants in South Africa*, the benchmark against which all other guides in South Africa must be measured. She is a force to be reckoned with. Her photograph is said to be pinned up in restaurant kitchens, under the warning, 'Beware!'

Matching wine and food is a particular passion of Jos's, but she approaches it from the very sensible viewpoint that 'You can change nothing in the bottle,' so it's the food that must be moulded to fit in with the wine.

An honorary Vigneron de Franschhoek, Jos is also founder and leader of the Cape Town Convivium of the international Slow Food movement. She has led tastings of South African wines at the largest gastronomic fair in Europe, the Salone del Gusto in Turin, and has represented South Africa at the Slow Food World Congress. She keeps in touch with food trends and indulges her palate at Michelin-starred restaurants in regular, restaurant-driven trips to Europe.

Slow Food is an international movement, with headquarters in Bra, Italy. It was started in 1986 in reaction to fast food, by Carlo Petrini, who was outraged when the golden arches of a well-known hamburger purveyor went up in Rome. There are now convivia in 45 countries with over 80 000 members. The amazing growth of the movement, and the fact that it is now a global force, shows the international sympathy for the aims of the organisation.

Slow Food's original aim focused on the biodiversity of the planet, with its priority being the preservation of the culinary past for future generations. It is anti pre-packaged, homogenised food – fast food that erodes culinary tradition. It promotes food that is grown and cooked with love and care. It believes in flavour, natural foodstuffs and fresh ingredients, rather than the convenience food that dominates today's eating patterns.

Slow Food today seeks to promote a new approach to gastronomy, through support of small farmers and a widespread education programme. President Carlo Petrini emphasises that food cannot be a source of pleasure unless it has been produced in a way that respects the environment, the land, the local traditions and the food culture of the various peoples involved.

Under Jos's leadership Slow Food in Cape Town aims to become a force for tradition and preservation in the Cape. The movement identifies and presents awards to artisanal producers annually. Among its noble intentions are the establishment of an 'Ark of Taste' and to identify and record threatened species. The Cape boasts an enormous wealth of indigenous plants and herbs, many of which need to be saved from extinction. Slow Food is also concerned about the environment. As Petrini says, you cannot be a true gourmet without being a conservationist. In an age when genetically modified foodstuffs are the norm, and animal fodder has caused illnesses such as mad cow disease, the movement supports organic farming and natural products like cheese from non-pasteurised milk.

The Cape Town Convivium has established the Funa Foods Fund (*funa* is an African word meaning 'needy'), directed at upliftment. The projects it supports are food-related and motivated from within the community.

In 1990, I had the amazing experience of working with the irrepressible and enthusiastic Michel Roux at The Waterside Inn at Bray. At the time it was a 3 Michelin star restaurant and a steep learning curve for me.

GRILLED FIGS WITH GOAT'S CHEESE AND SMOKED BEEF CRISP
Serves 6

I created this dish with European overtones in Cape Town and dedicate it to Jos, whom I regard as a living national treasure.

You'll need:

12 fresh figs

some olive oil

3 logs of plain chevin

6 slices of smoked beef

a handful of browned pine nuts

6 plain poppadums

interesting salad greens like
    watercress or wild rocket

extra virgin olive oil

balsamic vinegar

sea salt

freshly milled black pepper

Method: Cut the figs in half and spray with olive oil. Heat a ridged pan and brown the figs cut side down over high heat very quickly. Set aside. Place thick slices of the goat's cheese on a baking tray, spray with olive oil, brown under a hot grill and set aside. Scrunch up the slices of smoked beef, deep-fry quickly in oil till crisp, and drain on kitchen paper. Have the pine nuts ready. The poppadums can be cooked in the microwave, which makes them less fatty – works like a charm by the way. Now construct your salad. Toss the salad greens in olive oil and balsamic vinegar, season with the sea salt and freshly milled black pepper. Place the poppadum on a plate and pile the salad on top. Put two figs on each plate of salad and place the slices of goat's cheese in the spaces. Sprinkle with the pine nuts. Season – it's nice to use salt crystals from the West Coast and freshly ground black pepper.

Wine suggestion: One of my favourite wines is the Voyager Estate Semillon & Sauvignon Blanc blend from Western Australia. It is zesty and packed with fruity sauvignon, which is grown in a little patch of red gravelly loam not far from the ocean in Margaret River, with semillon to fill out the palate and add to the already jam-packed flavour spectrum. For the first time in 2004, the quality of the Voyager Sauvignon Blanc was so unique that viticulturist Steve James and award-winning winemaker Cliff Royle used a small percentage of it to produce a single-variety Voyager Estate Sauvignon Blanc 2004.

BUITENVERWACHTING CHRISTINE

It would be fair to call the Christine one of the foremost Bordeaux-style blends of the Cape. And coming from Constantia it has the unique attribute of that valley, the slow ripening of the vineyards shielded from the sun in the late afternoons.

Buitenverwachting is one of the architectural gems of Constantia, a proud manor house which faces the morning sun confident of its place in this amazingly beautiful valley. How beautiful it must have been before the development of the city, when from Ladies Mile towards False Bay the closest house would have been Bergvliet. I remember as a boy visiting relations in Constantia when most of it was still farmland.

There can be few occasions as unique as sitting with Jos Baker in the restaurant at Buitenverwachting, looking up towards the mountains over green vineyards, eating their chef's five-star food and drinking this wine, regarded by many as their favourite of its style.

It is a blend of the traditional Bordeaux varieties: cabernet sauvignon, cabernet franc, merlot and from the 1998 vintage, malbec. Herman Kirschbaum, winemaker at Buitenverwachting for more than 10 years, has gently tweaked the wine to a slightly more New World style, though the oaking in all-new French barrels – up to 30 months for some vintages – needs time to integrate into the wine.

It is well worth the detour to buy some of this wine and well worth the care to lay some down in ideal conditions for a later reward. It will be a pleasure delayed and *buiten verwachting* – beyond expectation.

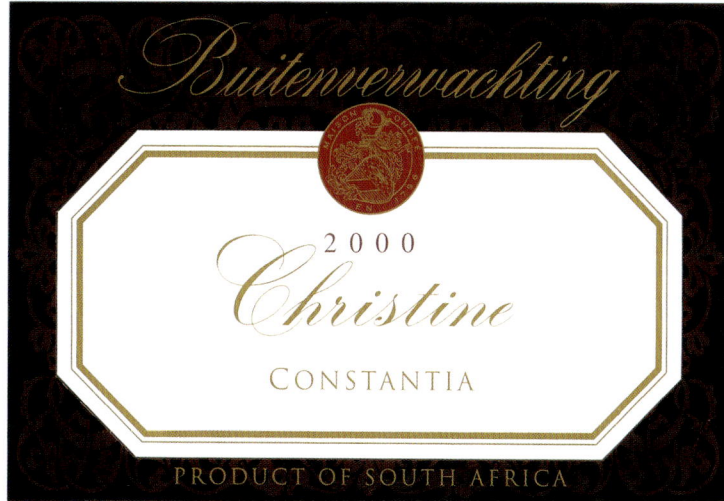

CHAPTER TWELVE

Paddagang – the Frog Passage

FOR A SHORT TIME IN THE LATE 1980s, Madeleine and I had a lease on Paddagang Restaurant on Tulbagh's Church Street. One of the enticements was that our friends Jan and Janey Muller lived there. They founded Lemberg Wine Estate and Janey made some very special wines there mainly from Hárslevelü, which she had planted on the recommendation of Desiderius Pongracz, and sauvignon blanc. Our sons, Peter and Josef, were both born when we lived in Tulbagh.

Parts of Tulbagh had been devastated by an earthquake on September 29, 1969. Gawie and Gwen Fagan, renowned Cape Town restoration architects, brought Church Street back to life by restoring the buildings back to their 18th- and 19th-century glory, among them Paddagang. The restaurant had been run by KWV for 14 years and Madeleine and I had a lot of fun restyling and repositioning it, and we were fortunate that in the first year we managed to double the number of people walking through the front door.

Paddagang was named after the frogs that used the one side of the property as a passage to and from Church Street, which had open gutters down each side of the road for the watering of gardens. There was an extremely large and long brown cobra that lived in the garden in front of the restaurant – sustained I am sure by a diet of frogs. Andries, my gardener, had a very gentle 'I live with it' attitude towards the creature.

Paddagang was well known for its Cape dishes, a tradition we kept up. Among these dishes was the bredie. Both the word and the stew are of Malay origin and very much a Cape dish. A bredie is a thick, fully flavoured meat stew, usually made from a fatty cut of lamb and named for the vegetable that is the other main ingredient, the potato, which usually thickened the sauce. The pot in which a bredie is cooked is shaken regularly, whether cooked on top or in the oven, because this helps to create an emulsified sauce. Green or dried beans, tomatoes, pumpkin and even quinces, cabbage or cauliflower are regular ingredients of bredies. Waterblommetjies (*Aponogeton distachyos*), a type of water hyacinth found in ponds and dams in the Cape in early spring, make a delicious bredie which is usually flavoured with wild sorrel juice, tangy and rich in Vitamin C. (Wild sorrel leaves, which contain oxalic acid, were also used in the early days of the Cape for cleaning the brass of measuring and jam-boiling utensils.)

Initially we decided to work on the dishes we wanted to use by deconstructing them and putting them together again using modern cooking methods and as many of the traditional flavourings and spices as possible. We were fortunate in having a great cook, now sadly deceased at far too young an age, called Netta Kok. She was a kind, loving, gentle soul who was such a great teacher to us and such a willing pupil for all the changes we wanted to make.

SNOEKSMOOR – BRAISED SNOEK
Serves 20 people as a first course and 10 as a main course.

Snoek is a member of the barracuda family and not always a trustworthy one! At times the hawkers who take it from the boats overhandle it, and the flesh is soft and pulpy. So be careful when you buy it fresh at the roadside. Here is our version of a traditional Cape snoek dish, perhaps in larger quantities than you might like it, but ingredients aren't carved in stone and you can happily halve them for fewer servings.

You'll need:

100 g unsalted butter

6 large onions, thinly sliced

6 large cloves garlic, peeled
  and chopped

4 chillies, sliced (leave in the seeds
  and veins if you like extra heat)

5 medium potatoes, peeled
  and quartered

2 large lemons

1 whole smoked snoek,
  uncoloured and lightly salted,
  soaked overnight in cold
  water if too salty

melted unsalted butter

1 x 250 ml tea cup filled with
  chopped parsley

sea salt if necessary

freshly milled black pepper

200 g melted unsalted butter

200 ml unsalted fish fumet
  or boiling water

Method: Melt the 100 g unsalted butter in a large frying pan over very low heat and, stirring occasionally, fry the onions, garlic and chilli, until the onion is a rich golden colour, starting to caramelise and soft. Do not hurry this process.

Peel and quarter the potatoes and boil them gently in a closed saucepan until done, ensuring that they stay whole. Grate the peel off the lemons with a fine grater, squeeze out the juice and set aside. Preset the grill. Preset the oven to 180 °C. Place the snoek on a baking tray, brush over the melted unsalted butter and grill until a good, rich golden colour. Remove the bones and break the snoek up into bite-sized pieces. In an ovenproof dish, place the snoek pieces, then the potatoes, sprinkle over half the parsley, all the lemon peel and some sea salt if you feel the need and freshly milled black pepper. Pour over the 200 ml melted butter, the fish fumet (or water) and the lemon juice, and top with the onions. Cover with foil and heat through in the preset oven.

When ready, toss gently to mix well and taste for final flavour adjustment. Sprinkle with the remaining parsley and serve on steamed white rice with wedges of lemon, fresh sliced chilli and sliced spring onions.

Wine suggestion: Adjacent to our farm was Altydgedacht, farmed by the Parker family. Today Oliver and John Parker make some exciting, innovative wines. I particularly like their Altydgedacht Barbera. Their Altydgedacht Gewürztraminer is dry with whiffs of jasmine and honeysuckle and delicious grapefruit skin oil, a perfect match for the Indian flavours of the dish.

WATERBLOMMETJIEBREDIE
Serves 12

This lamb dish is a great tradition in the Cape where waterblommetjies (*Aponogeton distachys*), also known as wateruintjies, fill the ponds and dams in the Western Cape with pretty, white, snowdrop-like, strongly scented flowers. C Louis Leipoldt, in his book on Cape cookery, refers to them in English as water hawthorn, and Myrna Robins, well-known Cape wine and food writer, as water hyacinth. They have a delicate flavour, like a cross between asparagus and artichoke hearts.

It is important that the flowers are just opening with the calices still bright green and firm. To prepare them, remove any of the black centres of the flowers. They need to be soaked in lots of salted water to remove any bugs and then rinsed through well in a couple of basins of freshly drawn water.

Maddy and I found it best to use a combination of thick rib – which adds a little flavourful fat to the dish – and lean shoulder. Many of the old Cape recipes advocate using a piece of sheep's tail to add a bit of fat, and others recommend a 'nice fat leg of lamb'.

You'll need:

6 medium onions, peeled and finely sliced

2 Tbs sunflower oil – more if you need it

3 small green chillies, seeded and chopped (leave in the seeds and veins for extra heat)

6 fat cloves garlic, peeled and chopped

3 fat slices of ginger, peeled

3 kg lamb, or young mutton, which is more flavourful – use 1 kg thick rib with bones and 2 kg boned shoulder

seasoned flour

sea salt

freshly milled black pepper

6 allspice berries

4 cloves

half a nutmeg, grated

250 ml full-bodied red wine

1 litre good beef stock or demi-glace

2 handfuls wild sorrel or lemon juice or tamarind juice

2 kg waterblommetjies, prepared as above

1 kg medium potatoes, peeled and quartered

1 Tbs soft brown sugar

*A basket of fresh
waterblommetjies.*

Method: In a heavy-bottomed ovenproof casserole with a tight-fitting lid, gently fry the onions in the oil. As they start turning golden, add the chillis, garlic and ginger and continue frying until the onions are light gold in colour. Remove and drain on kitchen paper. Dust the meat lightly in seasoned flour and brown in batches, keeping the temperature high. Keep the browned meat aside on a plate. Pour off any excess oil from the casserole and wipe out with a kitchen paper towel. Return the meat (with any juices which may have collected on the plate) and onion mixture to the casserole. Season well with sea salt, freshly milled black pepper and add the allspice berries, cloves and nutmeg. The berries and cloves can be put into a little muslin bag so that you can remove them later – awful to get a clove in your mouth!

If you like you can add half the blommetjies to the dish at this stage – they will cook very soft. Add the wine and stock and braise on top of the stove or in a 180 °C oven for 1½ hours. It is a good idea to cool the dish at this stage and refrigerate overnight to allow the flavours to mature. If you don't have the time, continue with the recipe.

The following day, lift any solidified fat off the top, and reheat the casserole gently. Place the sorrel, lemon juice or tamarind juice on top, then the blommetjies and finally the potato. Sprinkle over the sugar and spoon some of the sauce over the top. Steam, simmering gently for a further 1½ hours, either on top of the stove or in a 180 °C oven, by which time the potato will be cooked. When ready to serve, stir through gently and serve with steamed white rice and wedges of lemon.

Wine suggestion: You need a deliciously edgy and perfect pinotage with soft, ripe tannins and great fruit. The Kaapzicht Steytler Pinotage hits the button.

SAMOOSAS – VEGETARIAN VERSION
Serves 6 people

After bobotie, samoosas are one of the best-known Cape dishes, thought to have originated in India. The best ones I have ever eaten were from the little stalls on the Grand Parade in the city of Cape Town. As a boy I used to buy these while waiting for a bus to take me from my school, SACS, to the boarding house in the suburbs. As a special treat, when we had time, we used to walk up into District Six and buy even more yummy ones there. They could contain beef, chicken or a curried vegetable mix. Although available throughout the year, they are especially eaten on the morning of the Eid ul-Fitr feast at the end of the holy fasting month of Ramadan. The dough used is usually home-made and called *pur*.

When we are in Cape Town, we buy the best samoosas at The Avenue Café in Newlands from the Bahatkar brothers, whose family I have known for 35 years from the time that their business was run by their father and they were his young assistants. There must be very few people in Newlands who don't know The Avenue Café. For me, a visit there is like seeing old and loved friends. I remember, when she was a little girl, reading my daughter Sarah a children's story about where milk comes from. It went through the whole process from grass to bottle. At the end I asked her, 'Now darling, do you know where milk comes from?' 'Yes, Daddy,' was her reply, 'from Mr Bahatkar.'

This samoosa recipe was a result of much frying and baking in our house while we perfected it. The recipe gives you two options, one for frying and one for baking. I even took the recipe to Australia and served the samoosas in the restaurant on Voyager Estate for The Margaret River Wine Festival.

You'll need:

4 Tbs vegetable oil

1 large onion, chopped

2 cloves garlic, finely chopped

2cm fresh ginger, very finely chopped

1 fresh red chilli, finely chopped and add the seeds and
veins if you want some extra heat

6 spring onions, cut into slices – keep the green and
white parts separate

1 tsp curry powder or garam masala

½ tsp turmeric

½ tsp ground coriander

¼ tsp ground ginger

120 g potatoes, diced small

120 g carrots, diced small

tomato purée, to add moisture if necessary

100 g young spinach leaves, cooked and chopped

juice of half a lemon

small bunch fresh coriander leaves, finely chopped

6 sheets phyllo pastry (for baking) or spring-roll pastry
(for deep frying)

1 egg, beaten

Method: In the oil, fry the onion, garlic, ginger, chilli, the white parts of the spring onions and cook, stirring continuously, until the vegetables begin to colour. Add the spices and cook for a short while to release the aromatic oils. Add the diced potatoes, carrots and tomato purée if necessary. Continue to cook, stirring from time to time, until the moisture has almost evaporated and the mixture is cooked through. Now stir in the spinach, the green parts of the spring onions, the lemon juice and the coriander leaves. Cover the pan, remove from the heat and reserve.

Cut each phyllo or spring roll sheet in half lengthways. Fold both long sides of each piece of pastry over to the centre to make a narrow strip about 5 cm wide with two strengthening 'hems'. Place 2 teaspoons of the vegetable mixture at the top of a strip of pastry. Fold one corner over to make a triangle shape at the top, then turn the triangle over at the base, and continue to fold in the same way until you reach the end of the pastry strip and have a fat triangle-shaped samoosa. Brush the inside of the last fold of pastry with a little beaten egg with your finger and seal the samoosa.

Continue with the other pastry strips. Place the samoosas on a baking tray and reserve. If using phyllo pastry, preheat the oven to 180 °C. Bake the samoosas in the preheated oven for 25-30 minutes or until puffed and golden brown. If using spring-roll pastry, fry them in hot oil. The samoosas can be served immediately or allowed to cool and eaten later as a snack.

Wine suggestion: I often feel that people don't really take sherry sufficiently seriously. In South Africa, sadly, the number of producers is diminishing and while a company like Monis continues to win all sorts of awards, I don't believe sufficient is being done to keep this great tradition going. The wonderful nuttiness of the flor yeast and the contribution of the oak are to me unsurpassable. There are times for chilled sherry and this is one of them. We always offered sherry to guests arriving for lunch and served it in a clear glass decanter as an apéritif, the better to see its colour. While some like it dry, most would prefer not to have it too dry. We used the Douglas Green Flor Sherries at Paddagang – great quality that they sensibly sold in 2-litre screwcap bottles! Monis Medium Cream is a much-awarded Cape sherry – try it with the samoosas.

RAYMOND AND BETTY O'GRADY – Berries by Appointment

Maddy and I first met Raymond and Betty when we worked at Boschendal, where Raymond looked after personnel affairs. For a couple of years they lived next door to us on the farm and our children ran in and out of each other's houses. Raymond's garden always had several rows of trellises of a variety of berries from which he made what our daughter Amy called Raymond's Jam, and today my children enjoy no other.

Raymond and Betty now own Hillcrest Berry Orchards, at the top of the Helshoogte Pass near Stellenbosch. They produce a huge tonnage of berries each year – blueberries, raspberries of the red and gold variety, tayberries, blackberries and gooseberries. From these and other bought-in fruits they make a range of the most delicious and unique preserves and fruit-flavoured vinegars. They import and bottle red- and white-wine vinegar, sherry vinegar and also champagne vinegar. Their olive oils come from a small family business in Tuscany and some are flavoured with chilli and others with lemon. Their berries have graced the tables of many restaurants and were served to Queen Elizabeth and Prince Charles on visits to South Africa.

The tons of duck we roasted in our restaurants were coated in a berry-reduction sauce flavoured with crème de cassis and made from blackberries from Hillcrest Berry Orchards.

Maddy and I have stayed over in their guest cottages on the farm and have breakfasted in the restaurant on the estate, the veranda of which must have the best view in the country. Almost alpine, with towering mountains around it on all sides, it is a real treat.

The duck dish and the berry dessert we served at Parks Restaurant were used to highlight the wonderful Hillcrest berries.

Dermot, Raymond and Betty O'Grady, Amy, me, Peter, Maddy, Annie and Helène de Villiers.

DUCK WITH BLACKBERRY SAUCE
Serves 4

This recipe uses two ducks, each weighing about 2 kg. They are roasted, cut off the bone and the carcasses used in the making of the sauce. The demi-glace used should be made with beef or veal bones (this helps with the consistency of the final sauce and makes it easier for the butter to be held in emulsion, though you can cheat and use tinned, undiluted consommé), well reduced and flavoured lightly with tomato. Once the sauce is completed, the duck is crisped up under a hot grill and served on top of the sauce with a garnish of fresh blackberries.

You'll need:

300 g blackberries

20 g icing sugar

1 Tbs blackcurrant jam

5 Tbs red-wine vinegar flavoured
   with blackberries

2 Tbs crème de cassis

250 ml tomato-flavoured
   demi-glace

80 g unsalted butter cut into
   small blocks and kept cold
   on a plate in the fridge

sea salt

freshly milled black pepper

Method: In a small saucepan, cook the berries and the icing sugar with 50 ml water over high heat, uncovered, for about 5 minutes. Strain, reserving the juice for later use. Set aside the berries for use as a garnish. In a separate saucepan, stir the jam into the wine vinegar, reduce and caramelise. When dark brown, deglaze with the crème de cassis. Add the demi-glace, the chopped-up duck carcasses and the juice from the blackberries. Bring to the boil, lower the heat to very low and simmer, uncovered, for about 20 minutes, skimming off any foam on top. Strain carefully through a fine strainer into a small pan.

Over the lowest heat, whisk in the little blocks of butter, taking care not to raise the heat too much because this will cause the butter to oil and the sauce to split. Check the seasoning and reseason if necessary. Add the berries, but not any juice that might have accumulated around them. Grill the duck portions to crisp up the skin and heat through. Serve on a warm plate – not too hot as the sauce could split on it – with the duck on top of the sauce.

Wine suggestion: Slaley Shiraz would be perfect with this dish. The dark fruit and accessibility of the wine complement the flavours of the sauce.

BLUEBERRY CLOUDS
Serves 4

You'll need:

6 egg whites

pinch cream of tartar

300 g castor sugar

splash of Hillcrest Champagne
  Vinegar (or mild white-wine
  vinegar)

1 vanilla pod

30 g cornflour

seasonal blueberries

150 ml double cream

4 Tbs crème fraîche

icing sugar

Method: Preset the oven to 120 °C. Whisk the egg whites and the cream of tartar with an electric beater till they form soft peaks. Add the sugar, vinegar, the seeds from the vanilla pod and the corn flour, and mix for a further minute. Use the pod to make vanilla sugar. Spoon four large egg shapes onto non-stick baking paper and make a small 'dam' in the top for the filling. Bake in the preset oven for about 40 minutes until the outside is crispy and the centre is still soft. Leave to cool. When cool these meringues can be stored in an airtight container.

To serve, flood the plate with some fresh blueberry coulis, place the meringue on it and then spoon the crème fraîche and a spoonful of berries on top of each meringue, top with whipped cream and dust with icing sugar and serve with extra blueberries.

My beautiful wife and me at the opening of Paddagang on December 4, 1985.

PIERRE JOURDAN, MÉTHODE CAP CLASSIQUE

I don't think Achim von Arnim would mind my telling you that he is a larger than life fella. Even if he sat quietly in the corner of a room (he would not be able to do this mind you!), his mere presence would fill it. Achim is a different kettle of fish. He is passionate, almost more passionate than I have ever come across in a human being, dedicated, more hardworking than most, focused so completely to achieve his mission, and – my favourite characteristic – available: to new ideas, to explore, to the breaking down of barriers, to new wine styles.

It's not surprising therefore that he should choose the Cape version of champagne – Méthode Cap Classique. A noisy wine to start with, it becomes even more so in the opening thereof by sabrage, done by Achim in grand style, using a French cavalryman's sword, after his traditional Saturday morning cellar tour. One of the enchanting things about Achim is that he will offer the opportunity to open a bottle to an elderly lady – he wouldn't get a kiss from an elderly man! – and make a uniquely special moment for her. I saw him lining up the bottles once at the wedding of a mutual friend where his wine was being served, ready for their decapitation. His bubbly is an alive wine with a soft gentle mousse and delicate bubbles rising to the top, a wine of colour, from the delicate straw of the Brut to the strawberry overtones of the Belle Rose.

All of Achim's sparkling wines can face up to almost any food on the menu. He produces a superb benchmark South African pinot noir under the Haute Cabrière label, a delicious 'non-sparkling champagne' called Tranquille and a sweet chardonnay called Ratafia which is fortified by Achim's own estate chardonnay brandy. So he covers all bases on the menu.

CHAPTER THIRTEEN

Parks Restaurant – us at our best

PARKS RESTAURANT WAS A DREAM AND A PASSION FOR DALE PARKER, ITS OWNER. We were fortunate to be part of that dream for nine years until Dale's untimely death in 2001.

We were fortunate, too, to employ over the years an amazing group of people, many of whom have gone on to great things in Europe and worked for people like Marco Pierre White, Gary Rhodes, Gordon Ramsay and others of their ilk. We were patronised by what must surely be the most thoroughly decent, loyal, supportive and loving guests, Dale and Elizabeth Parker among them – they dined at their special table we kept in the sitting room should we ever be fully booked when they wanted to eat there. Many of the guests became loved friends and will remain so for the rest of our lives.

Parks Restaurant was housed in a restored Edwardian suburban villa in Wynberg, Cape Town. Dale employed

Us ... older and wiser.

David van den Heever, a restoration architect who sympathetically, though taking into consideration its use as a restaurant, returned the house to its original glory. Jay Smith, one of Cape Town's top interior designers, created an atmosphere that literally took people's breath away as they came through the front door. Patricia Fraser's graphics were quirky yet in superb taste. Sandi Eastwood adorned the walls with the most eclectic and contemporary works of art.

Parks played to a full house from the day it opened in July 1993 to the day it closed in April 2002 with much popping of champagne and shedding of tears.

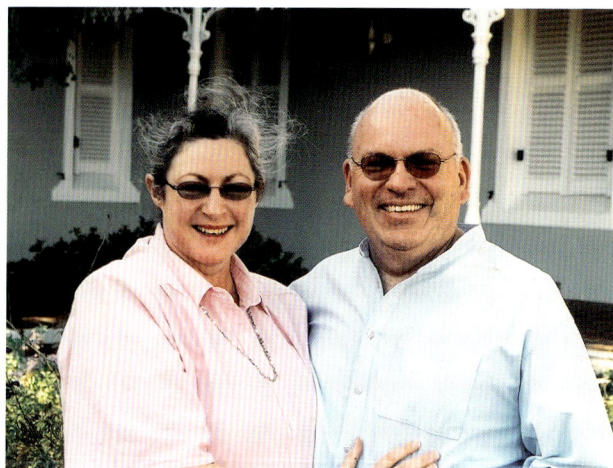

It was the most unique and special time of our lives. We were nominated in the national Top Ten Restaurants, were awarded a Blazon by the prestigious Chaîne des Rôtisseurs and were the subject of numerous complimentary reviews and accolades.

The spirit of Parks left with Maddy and me and we still hold it dear to our hearts. We miss the people, our wonderful staff and guests, but quite frankly I don't miss the late nights and the relentlessness of the restaurant business!

Here is a selection of recipes from our kitchen, which Maddy and I styled and our innovative and creative chefs made their own.

Our beautiful Parks Restaurant, at the bottom of Wynberg Hill.

Left: Me and the family on our last night at Parks.
Below: Amy, Maddy, Elizabeth and Dale Parker and Sandi and Jane Eastwood.
Far below: Parks staff at a Christmas gathering.

PAN-GRILLED CALAMARI TUBES ON A RISOTTO CAKE WITH CHILLI, LEMON & BALSAMIC DRESSING
Serves 6

You'll need:

12 medium calamari tubes,
    cleaned

For the dressing, you'll need:

3 red chillies, finely chopped
100 ml balsamic vinegar
200 ml olive oil
juice of 2 small lemons or
    limes, zest of one
sea salt and freshly ground
    black pepper

For the risotto, you'll need:

1 litre fish or vegetable stock
120 g butter
2 tbsp olive oil
1 medium onion, chopped
300 g arborio rice
sea salt
freshly ground black pepper
freshly grated Parmesan

fresh coriander for garnishing

Method: Cut each calamari tube down one side and open it out so that it forms a single layer. Score finely on each side (this will prevent shrinkage, which makes the calamari tough). Prepare the dressing by blending together the ingredients. If you do it in a blender, it will form a better emulsion. Leave in the chilli seeds and veins if you want a bit more heat. Marinate the calamari tubes in the dressing for a minimum of 2 hours.

Prepare the risotto by heating the fish stock. Check for seasoning and keep it hot. Melt 75 g of the butter with the oil in a heavy-based pot. Fry the onion until soft and transparent. Add the rice and stir to coat thoroughly with the oil. Add 2 ladles of the hot stock and stir while simmering as the rice absorbs the liquid; continue until all the liquid is absorbed. The stirring helps create the emulsion and produces a rich sauce. The rice should be cooked just beyond al dente. Check for seasoning and add a generous sprinkling of Parmesan cheese.

Spread the risotto onto a baking tray to a thickness of about 2 cm and allow to cool. When cold, cut into rings with a 6-cm cutter and fry gently in the remaining butter. Remove the calamari from the marinade. Pan-grill very quickly in a very hot, ridged, grill pan. Serve on top of a hot risotto cake, douse with some of the dressing and garnish with fresh coriander.

Wine suggestion: This dish, with its cross-cultural Pacific Rim calamari and Italian risotto-with-a-difference, is perfectly matched with the Neil Ellis Groenekloof Sauvignon Blanc.

STICKY TOFFEE PUDDING
Serves 6 – or 4 in our house

Jill Walsh, a young Irish woman, swept like a breath of fresh air through the kitchen of Parks for all too short a time in the late 1990s. She is one of the most hardworking and professional chefs I have employed. Jill, who had worked for Darina Allen at Ballymaloe Cookery School in Cork, brought an exciting traditional Irish edge to what we did in the kitchen at Parks, which many of our guests enjoyed. Her Ballymaloe Vinaigrette was very popular and a great discussion point on the menu. She worked for us at the time that this dessert was all the rage. And in our house it still is. That she left us her recipe for this pudding never quite made up for the gap she left in our lives.

For the cake, you'll need:
250 g chopped dates
300 ml tea
100g unsalted butter
175 g castor sugar
3 eggs
250 g self-raising flour
1 tsp bicarbonate of soda
1 tsp vanilla essence
1 tsp espresso coffee powder

For the hot toffee sauce,
   you'll need:
100 g butter
175 g soft brown sugar
100 g white sugar
285 g golden syrup
250 ml cream
½ tsp vanilla essence

Method: Set the oven to 180 °C. Brush a 20-cm springform cake tin with oil, line the base with a circle of greaseproof paper and oil again. Soak the dates in hot tea for 15 minutes and drain. Cream together the butter and the sugar until light and fluffy. Beat in the eggs one by one and then fold in the sifted flour. Add the bicarb, vanilla essence and the coffee to the dates, and fold into the mixture. Turn into the lined cake tin and bake for 1-1½ hours or until a skewer comes out clean.

For the hot toffee sauce, put the butter, brown and white sugar and the golden syrup into a saucepan and melt gently over low heat. Simmer for about 5 minutes, remove from the heat and gradually stir in the cream and the vanilla essence. Return to the heat and stir for 2-3 minutes or until the sauce is smooth.

To serve: put some of the sauce onto a serving plate, place a slice of the pudding on the sauce and pour more sauce over the top. Serve with the remaining sauce and softly whipped cream.

GROUNDNUT STEW
Serves 4

While we were at Parks, our son Peter announced that he was to become a vegetarian. Quite something for a boy of nine! He took us on a mystical magical trip through vegetarianism for the next 3½ years. It also made our vegetarian selection a lot more interesting than most restaurants had on offer in Cape Town at the time. This was a very popular dish with our vegetarian and even some carnivorous guests. The vegetable measurements are approximate and you can really use whatever you have available.

You'll need:

3 large sweet potatoes, cut into
    bite-sized cubes

olive oil

3 cloves garlic, finely chopped

3 Tbs grated fresh ginger, finely
    chopped

8 medium onions, chopped

2 Tbs ground coriander

½ tsp cayenne pepper

2 skinned tomatoes

4 x 250 ml cups aubergine, cubed

1 x 250 ml cup courgettes, cubed

2 large red peppers, cut in
    julienne strips

400 ml tomato juice

3 Tbs peanut butter

peanuts for garnish

Method: Boil or bake the sweet potatoes until tender. Sauté the garlic, ginger and onion until transparent and just browning. Add the spices and stir for a few moments to release the flavours. Add the tomatoes and aubergine with a small amount of water and simmer for about 5 minutes. Add the courgettes and peppers and braise gently until cooked. Drain the sweet potatoes and add, with the tomato juice and peanut butter. Stir well and simmer for 5 minutes, stirring to prevent the mixture from sticking.

Wine suggestion: The Diners' Club Young Winemaker of the Year 2004 was a young man from Darling, called Johan Nesenberend, and the wine a 2002 shiraz, called For My Friends. It is a full, soft, aromatic shiraz that would accompany this dish perfectly.

SPICY FISH CAKES WITH THAI-STYLE DIPPING SAUCE
Serves 4

A lot of jokes were made about me serving fish cakes in a fine restaurant. Once we even did them about the size of ping-pong balls and served them with fried parsley and tartare sauce.

For the fish cakes, you'll need:
500 g white fish, skin off, filleted
   and cut into blocks
1 Tbs Thai fish sauce
2 small red chillies, seeded and
   chopped
finely grated lemon or lime rind
1 Tbs chopped fresh coriander
1 egg
1 Tbs soft brown sugar
½ tsp salt
50 g very finely sliced green beans
sea salt
freshly ground black pepper

For the dipping sauce, you'll need:
3 Tbs Thai fish sauce
3 Tbs freshly squeezed lemon or
   lime juice
2 Tbs sugar or more to taste
3 Tbs water
1 clove garlic, crushed
4 hot red or green chillies

Method: For the fish cakes, place all the ingredients into a food processor and process until smooth. Add the green beans. Fry off a small piece to test for seasoning and adjust by adding sea salt and freshly milled pepper or more chilli if desired. This amount of mixture should make about 16 cakes, depending on the size you desire. Make up the mixture into fish cakes and fry in hot oil (sunflower or canola, not olive) for about 1 minute on each side. Drain on paper towels.

For the dipping sauce, mix together the ingredients other than the chillies. Cut the chillies into thin rounds (removing the seeds) and divide them among four small glass bowls. Pour the dipping sauce over the chillies and serve with the fish cakes.

Wine suggestion: Pieter 'Bubbles' Ferreira was the Diners' Club Winemaker of the Year 2004 for his 1998 Blanc de Blancs bubbly. His has a wonderful way with non-bubbly wines too. In the Graham Beck Chardonnay he manages to retain fresh fruit with strong citrus overtones and delicious fat vanilla from the oak barrels. It's nice and crisp too to cut through the fish cakes. Pieter's greatest asset is his totally enchanting wife, Ann, whose mother, Adré McWilliam-Smith, is mentioned elsewhere in this book. His 12-year-old son, William, has already made his first wine – called No Way Rosé.

ANNETTE LE ROUX – 5-star Chef of the Karoo

'My sister is a chef and she has just returned from New Zealand and is looking for a job for the season.' Thus spoke Emelia Smuts, to whom I spoke whenever I ordered Groot Constantia Wine from the estate for Parks Restaurant.

It so happened that it was coming up for Christmas and we were short of one person on the kitchen team. Annette le Roux came to work for us the next week. This started a friendship not only with her, but also with her entire family. And a large family it is too.

Annette comes from a farm called Doornkraal, near De Rust in the Klein Karoo. De Rust, 'the rest' or 'resting-place', would have been a stopping place to rest one's horses after or before passing through Meiringspoort, a spectacular portal through the Swartberg onto the plains of the Great Karoo. Annette's family has farmed there for generations, her father, popularly known as Swepie, being the current incumbent. Swepie has been a mover and shaker in the agricultural and especially the wine industry, in a wine appellation region known as the Klein Karoo.

Ann is the chatelaine of a large, rambling, welcoming home, the kitchen of which hums with activity. This is a real farm kitchen which makes use of every fruit and vegetable produced in its vast kitchen garden. The citrus orchard has unusual fruits, like shaddock, from which Ann makes the most delicious 'Bitter Syrup', a limey, lemony cordial with a refreshing, bitter aftertaste. When I call, I am often told: 'Ann is making strawberry jam', 'Ann is making green fig preserve', or 'Ann has just finished a batch of chilli jam'.

Annette quietly worked her magic in the Parks Restaurant and at the same time worked her way into our hearts. Supremely talented, good food seemed to come out of the ends of her fingers. She enchanted our children too.

Annette and Celia opened their restaurant Jemima's, in Baron van Rheede Street in Oudtshoorn, about five years ago. It is housed in a quaint stone house with a veranda on the street onto which tables spill on warm, windless, summer nights. They proceeded to make it a legend, being nominated among the country's top 10 restaurants and appearing in the *Top 100 Restaurants Guide* issued by *Wine* magazine each year. In 2004, this guide gave her a '5-star chef' award.

Annette's pumpkin pie is deliciously savoury and a vegetarian hit at Jemima's. The riper the butternut, the better tasting the pie.

120

ANNETTE LE ROUX'S PUMPKIN PIE
Serves 8 portions for hungry diners

Trust Annette to add her unique twist to a recipe. When you think of Pumpkin Pie, you think of a cinnamony dessert. Hers is deliciously savoury and a vegetarian's dream dish. This one is a great hit at Jemima's. The riper the butternut, the better tasting the pie.

For the crust you'll need:
200 g cake flour
pinch sea salt
120 g cold butter
70 g grated Parmesan
pinch paprika
1 or 2 ice blocks

For the filling you'll need:
2 kg butternut, peeled, cut into
    blocks and boiled, which renders
    about 1.8 kg cooked weight
3 egg yolks
2 whole eggs
1 Tbs cornflour
½ tsp nutmeg, freshly and finely
    grated
½ tsp ground cinnamon
1 tsp ground cumin
sea salt
freshly milled black pepper

zest of 1 orange, grated finely
250 ml cream
350 g grated mozzarella cheese
350 g feta cheese, crumbled
375 ml Bulgarian yoghurt
2 eggs
1 large clove garlic, crushed
½ tsp turmeric
4 ripe sweet peppers, roasted and
    skinned (Annette uses 2 red and
    2 yellow)
3 Tbs dried breadcrumbs

Method: To make the crust, place all ingredients except the ice into the bowl of a food processor, using the dough blade. Blitz until the mixture resembles breadcrumbs. Add one ice block and blitz again. If necessary, add the second block of ice to bring the dough together. Roll the dough into a ball, wrap in plastic wrap and refrigerate.

Place the cooked butternut, egg yolks, eggs, cornflour, spices, orange rind and cream into the bowl of a food processor and blend until smooth. Turn into a mixing bowl and blend in the mozzarella and feta cheeses. Rinse out the food processor bowl and place in it the Bulgarian yoghurt, eggs, garlic, turmeric and sweet peppers, and blitz until smooth.

Preset the oven to 160 °C. Roll out the dough on a floured board and use it to line a prepared 28-cm springform cake tin. Place in the fridge for a few minutes and then bake blind in the preset oven until the crust is a light golden brown. Pour in the pumpkin filling, sprinkle the breadcrumbs on top and smooth over the red-pepper mixture.

Bake for 2 hours in the preset oven; cover with foil should it start browning on top. Serve hot or cold.

Annette serves this pie hot with brown butter sage sauce and a salad. Heat butter in a pan and fry in it some sage leaves till the butter turns golden brown, then season with sea salt and freshly milled black pepper. For restaurant service she garnishes the dish with deep-fried butternut strips. These are peeled from a butternut with a potato peeler and fried in oil which is not too hot.

Wine suggestion: At Domein Doornkraal, Annette's brother Piet and sister Maria make some pretty special wines. Choice for this dish could be the Doornkraal Kuierwyn – a chenin blanc, colombar and muscat blend, off-dry and medium-bodied, or Doornkraal Merlot – soft and mouthfilling with the guts to cut through the richness.

MULDERBOSCH CHARDONNAY

Maddy and I have loved this wine from soon after we opened Parks Restaurant, when the earlier vintages were on the market. We loved the visits by winemaker Mike Dobrovic and his passion for what he does. The Mulderbosch wines are quite uniquely labelled in that they have a thin strip of a label running down the side of the bottle. This alone makes them stand out on the store shelves.

Mike's chardonnay is a full, fat, creamy, buttery wine helped along by fermenting a portion of the wine in new and used barrels, which gives it the overtones of savoury vanilla and toffee. Mike blends in a percentage of tank-fermented chardonnay, which adds to the wine's flavour a bracing citrus edge, ripe summer melon, William pear and fat sun-ripened figs.

There is another Mulderbosch Chardonnay which is fermented in the barrel only and which is a huge rabble-rouser, rather like the captain of a pirate ship – all sorts of bluster, awash with fruit and pulled taffy, and walk-the-plank oak from mainly new French oak barrels.

It would not be right to leave out the Mulderbosch Faithful Hound, named for a dog that waited for its master who had died. This tail-wagging, friendly, dark-red-berry wine with accessible, soft tannins is made from five of the Bordeaux grape varieties, gently brushed with fine oak. Its enchanting, more conventionally shaped label is in the pastoral style with a hound that looks as if it had walked out of a Constable painting.

123

Maddy's food for boys

With our son, Peter, being a junior Western Province rower, we have a gang of young men – Roland, Justin, Bobby and others – who spend time in our home, either on their way to a rowing regatta or exhausted after it. Another thing they have in common is their love for Maddy's comfort food – large bowls of it.

Pasta is an important component because 'carbo-loading' in large measure is required the night before a regatta.

These are some of Madeleine's recipes that find great favour with the guys.

Da Boyz - Bobby Swallow, Tyrone Delaney, Peter, Justin 'Jubbs' Groenewald and Roland.

TOMATO PASTA SAUCE

You'll need:

4 large onions, finely chopped

2-4 Tbs good extra virgin olive oil

4 cloves garlic (if the rowers don't like garlic, leave it out)

4 x 410 g tins Italian chopped tomatoes, or 12 large, fresh, very ripe tomatoes

1-2 tsp sugar

sea salt

freshly milled pepper

4 long strips fresh oregano (more if you like) – we tend to put the whole stalk in; of course you can use dried – about 2 heaped teaspoons)

Method: Slowly brown the onions in the oil, then add the garlic for a few minutes before adding all the ingredients. Bring to a rapid boil, turn the heat down very low and allow to simmer for a good 2 hours or up to another hour depending on how reduced you want the sauce. What you don't use, freeze in portions for another day.

SAUCE BOLOGNAISE

For the above amount of tomato sauce, use 2 kg good-quality steak mince. Employ the method above, but before adding the tomatoes, sugar, salt and pepper and oregano, add the crumbled mince to the browned onion and garlic and stir-fry over high heat until lightly browned and natural liquid from the meat has evaporated. Proceed with the recipe by simmering gently for 3 hours or more depending on how reduced you want it. Re-season before using.

The above recipe will feed 12 hungry boys. You will need 3 x 500 g dried weight spaghetti for every 12 boys and grated cheese on the side. Serve with French loaves and a simple salad of lettuce, chunks of fresh tomatoes, cucumber and feta.

CHICKEN AND PENNE PASTA
Serves 6

You'll need:

24 rashers of bacon cut into strips

6 chopped onions

12 chicken breasts cut into strips

400 g large white button mushrooms, sliced

extra virgin olive oil

250 ml cream

sea salt

freshly milled black pepper

Method: Brown the bacon and remove from pan with slotted spoon. Brown the onions in the remaining bacon fat, adding a little olive oil if necessary. Fry the mushrooms to drive off as much moisture as possible. Remove from the pan with a slotted spoon. Stir-fry the chicken-breast strips in the remaining oil over high heat for a few minutes. Remove with the slotted spoon. Add all the cooked ingredients and the cream, salt and pepper, and heat through. (Add a little chicken stock if the sauce is not moist enough for the pasta.) Serve over cooked penne with rolls and salad.

Instead of breasts, you could use 3 deboned skinned chicken thighs per person and increase the cooking time by 20-30 minutes.

The four of us - not often together but always the happier for it. Me, Helen and Lilla, with Geoff at the back.

MADDY'S CHICKEN THIGH AND CHICK PEA CURRY
Serves 6

You'll need:

about 1 kg boned and skinned
   chicken thighs

2 Tbs sunflower oil

2 medium onions, peeled and
   roughly chopped

2 cloves garlic, peeled and
   chopped

3 Tbs medium curry powder

1 Tbs turmeric

2 Tbs white vinegar

1 Tbs sugar

1 x 410 g tin peeled chopped
   tomatoes

1 Tbs dried mixed herbs

4 Tbs peach chutney

2 bay leaves

250 ml chicken stock

1 x 410 g tin coconut milk

500 g carrots, peeled and cut into
   thumb-sized chunks

6 medium potatoes, peeled and
   quartered

sea salt

freshly milled black pepper

1 x 410 g tin chickpeas, drained

chopped fresh coriander

Method: Preset the oven to 180 °C. Wash the thighs and dry on kitchen paper. Heat the oil in an ovenproof casserole and in it, brown the onions slowly. Almost at the end of the browning process add the garlic and simmer a short while. Add the curry powder and turmeric and cook for 5 minutes to release the aromatic flavours. Add the vinegar and allow it to cook away. Add the sugar, tomato, herbs, chutney and the bay leaves. Add the chicken thighs and turn them gently in the mixture to coat thoroughly. Add the chicken stock and coconut milk, carrots and potatoes. Season well, bring to a simmer and then pop into oven for one hour with no lid on. Add the drained chickpeas, stir through gently and allow to heat with a lid on for 15 minutes. Sprinkle with the chopped coriander and serve with basmati rice and sambals.

Our beloved Amy as many of our Paddagang guests will remember her, usually dressed up as a rabbit or a cheetah. Wispy hair lovingly done by Geta Finlayson whose husband Peter always refers to her as the daughter I never had!

MADELEINE'S VEAL STOO
Serves 6

You'll need:

16 slices of veal shin

seasoned flour

50 ml olive oil

50 g butter

2 medium onions, roughly
   chopped

6 fat cloves garlic, peeled and
   sliced

2 Tbs snipped fresh sweet basil
   leaves

1 Tbs fresh oregano leaves

2 x 410 g tins chopped tomatoes
   (Italian preferably)

1 x 115 g tin tomato paste

500 ml dry white wine

500 ml good beef stock (use Ina
   Paarman's Beef Stock Powder)

salt

freshly milled black pepper

handful of chopped, flat-leaf
   parsley

grated rind of a large lemon

Method: Preset the oven to 180 °C. Snip the membrane round the edges of the veal shins to stop them from curling up. Dust the veal shin lightly with the seasoned flour and brown well under the grill on both sides – this keeps the fat content of the dish down. In an ovenproof casserole, heat together the olive oil and the butter, and in it colour the onions and garlic a delicate brown. Pour off as much fat as possible – blot up with some kitchen towel if necessary – and add the herbs, tomatoes, tomato paste, white wine and the beef stock. Bring to the boil and simmer uncovered for about 15 minutes. Season well with the sea salt and freshly milled black pepper. Bury the veal shin in the sauce, put on a lid and cook in the preset oven for about 90 minutes. Remove the lid and cook for a further 30 minutes. When the veal is very tender, you may remove it from the casserole and cook down the sauce to concentrate its flavour. Check again for seasoning, pour the sauce over the veal and garnish with the parsley and the lemon rind.

All the above are served with generous bowls of vegetables, pots of creamed spinach made with sautéed onions and cream, wokfuls of stir-fried vegetables, stoneware dishes of roasted butternut and sweet potato, wedges of fried potato, courgettes cooked quickly and at high heat in olive oil, and steamed broccoli and cauliflower. Result? Happy rowers!

THE BLUE CRANEFARM STALL AND OTHER FOOD EXPERIENCES

Over the last few years, when we have made our way eastwards to Sedgefield, we have planned our trip to include a meal with Theo and Jenny Pienaar at their Blue Crane Farmstall on the western side of Heidelberg, Cape. They are never closed and they are always both there. The menu offers perfect stopover food. Our favourite is the sandwiches made from Theo's fresh home-made breads and served with sensational potato salad and coleslaw and always a fruit salad using perfectly ripe fruits of the season. There is an embarrassment of riches in the jams, pickles, honeys, dried fruits, preserves and sauces department, most with their own label, and you will always find moskonfyt – a boiled grape syrup that we loved eating as children, poured onto fresh bread – and prickly pear syrup, which somehow made the thick buttermilk pancakes of our childhood so special that we could not have one without the other. Theo bakes all their breads – never less than a variety of six – and a selection of rusks that we buy to remind us for weeks afterwards of our stopover. I saw a packet of roasted unsalted peanuts there once and bought them to make a satay-type sauce and landed up with this recipe. It is a fusion of flavours from Indonesia, North Africa and my kitchen!

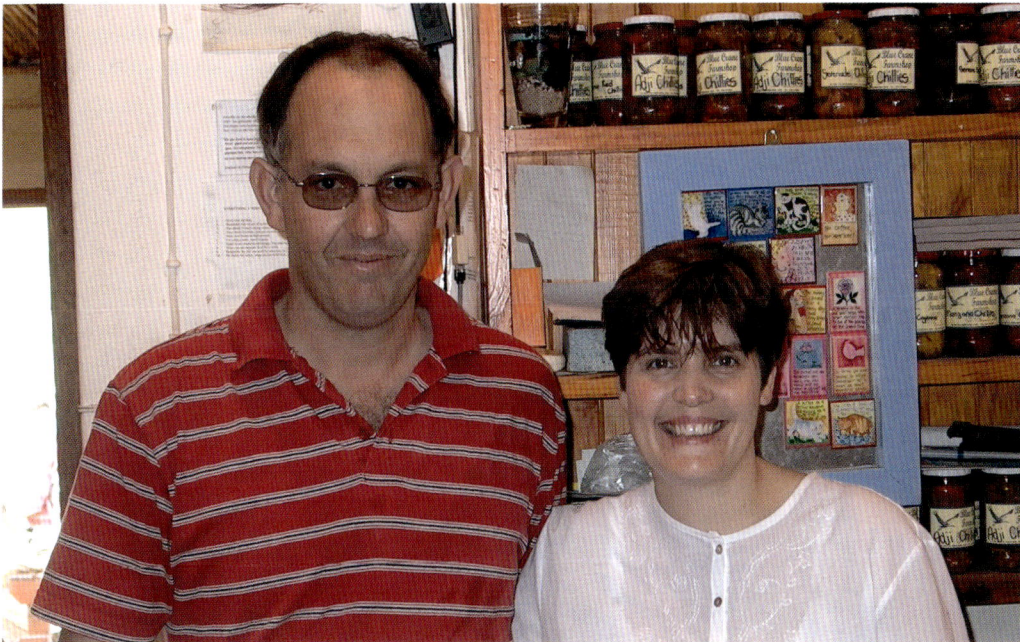

Theo and Jenny Pienaar, hardworking owners of Blue Crane - the 'must-stop' farmstall on the Garden Route.

129

CHICKEN BREASTS WITH PEANUT SATAY SAUCE
Serves 4

You'll need:

4 skinned and boned chicken
  breasts
Kikkoman soy sauce
mirin (or medium sherry)
rice or wine vinegar
250 g whole roasted unsalted
  peanuts
3 medium onions (300 g), finely
  chopped
3 fat cloves garlic, finely chopped
a little sunflower oil
2 Tbs tamarind paste
4 Tbs hot water
1 tin (400 ml) coconut milk
50 g finely chopped palm (or
  dark brown) sugar
4 tsp hot harissa, chilli powder
  or hot smoked paprika
fresh coriander, for a garnish

Method: Wash the chicken breasts, pat them dry with kitchen paper and bash out thinly with a mallet between sheets of plastic wrap. Score on the skin side with the point of a sharp knife – this will prevent shrinking when cooking. Mix equal small amounts of the soy sauce, mirin or sherry and vinegar, and marinate the chicken breasts in the mixture for about 2 hours. Set aside 50 g of the whole peanuts as a garnish and blitz the remainder in a food processor till fairly fine. Meantime make the sauce.

Cook the onion and garlic slowly in a little sunflower oil till golden brown. I found that stirring all the time helped to prevent it from sticking and I could use less oil. Add the tamarind paste, water, coconut milk, palm or brown sugar and as much or as little of the hot spice of your choice. Bring to the boil, turn down the heat and cook gently for about 10 minutes to cook through. The sauce can stand, covered, until required. Gently and quickly, fry the chicken breasts in a non-stick pan with very little oil. Reheat the sauce. Serve on some steamed white rice sprinkled with the remaining peanuts and some fresh coriander.

Wine recommendation: An off-dry wine with some peachy muscat characteristics, such as Villiera Sonnet.

GALETTE OF FRESH DATES WITH CARAMEL SAUCE
Serves 8

I am very fond of dates and lately there have been some delicious Medjool-type dates that come from Pella on the banks of the Orange River. I bought some of these at Blue Crane once and made a dessert that found its way on to the Parks Restaurant menu.

For the caramel sauce, you'll need:
500 g butter
300 g palm sugar
500 g dark brown sugar

For the galettes, you'll need:
500 g puff pastry
castor sugar
24 fresh pitted dates
thick cream

Method: Make the sauce. Combine all the ingredients in a medium saucepan and melt over a low heat, stirring until combined. Bring to the boil and cook for 10 minutes until reduced and thickened. Set aside to cool.

Make the galettes. Preheat the oven to 190 °C. Roll out the pastry and cut 8 x 8 cm discs. Place on a baking tray. Brush with water and sprinkle lightly with castor sugar. Bake in the oven for approximately 10 minutes or until risen and golden brown.

To serve: Heat the caramel sauce, roll the dates in the sauce and spoon three dates into each galette. Spoon over extra sauce and serve at once with whipped cream.

Wine suggestion: Two enchanting muscadels from Weltevrede Wine Estate in Bonnievale – Oupa se Wyn, which is their red muscadel, and Ouma se Wyn, a white. Both are rich, voluptuous and velvety smooth with waves of raisin, honey, dried fruit and hot almond brioche. Oupa se Wyn is made from an old bush-vine vineyard that was planted in 1926 by owner Lourens Jonker's grandfather – Oupa – and is a declared National Monument.

VRIESENHOF PINOT NOIR

If a gentle forested mountain could appear in human form it would appear as Jan Coetzee, a former world-class rugby player, whose legs still resemble the goal posts he aimed for in his years as a member of the team. They are often on view, because Jan is a resolute wearer of shorts to functions where his peers wear what they consider to be more formal attire. And seldom does he wear a jersey when the cool autumn winds blow up from the Antarctic. He personifies wine culture in South Africa and embraces wine production holistically with dignity and grace, like an elder statesman. Whenever I see him I feel a smile coming on.

He consults for other wineries, so his 'godchildren' appear wearing other colours, but it is in his own terroir on home soil that he excels. Jan is a passionate Burgundian and has spent time making wine there and applying his knowledge of Burgundian grapes to his winemaking processes here. We'd tasted his chardonnays with their wonderful oaky aromas and their chalky, mineral, citrus butter palates. He was more than well known for his pinotages even before he came to Vriesenhof. His cabernets – taking him away to Bordeaux from his Burgundian leanings – are elegant and classical with broad blackberry flavours, anise and fennel seed painted in as a faint cloud on the horizon and the other classical attributes of the cigar humidor and fine Cuban tobacco backing up the excellent oaking Jan gives his wines. Restrained and uptight in their youth, they become wondrous wines as they mature.

But for me it is Jan's Vriesenhof Pinot Noir that hits the spot. It took 22 years to make, from Dijon clones planted on different soil types, to achieve exactly the effect he wanted. I remember when the first vintage was released, how 'expected' it was. How beautifully packaged it was in its heavy Burgundy-shaped bottles with a classically French label, in elegant flat boxes.

Its aroma and flavour profile are classical and elegant too. The first time I tasted this wine, we used tall, elegant glasses, and as the wine gurgled from the bottle it looked like liquid ruby, well coloured but with the translucency one expects from a lady like pinot. Before you lift your glass the first layers of this multifaceted wine – fragrant, ripe, black Morello cherry and sappy sweet strawberry – reach out and lead you to the wine and its perfectly complementary aromas of toasted oak, farmyard and forest floor.

You need a quiet moment to take in all these gentle nudges to your senses.

A miscellany of recipes

CAPE MALAY PICKLED FISH
Serves 6 as a main course or 10 as a first course

On a visit to Voyager Estate in Western Australia, for The Margaret River Wine Festival, I wanted to serve pickled fish in the award-winning restaurant there. This is a dish of my childhood and one that is quintessentially Cape. Few Cape homes would not have their own recipe for *kerrievis* ('curried fish') because pickling was a popular way of preserving fish in the days before refrigerators. Often served as a first course, pickled fish also makes a main course with a salad of potato and accompanied by some dressed lettuce leaves.

You'll need:
2 kg fillet of firm white fish, all
   bones removed and cut into
   squares of about 6 cm
well-seasoned flour
125 ml vegetable oil

For the pickle, you'll need:
4 large onions, peeled, cut in half
   and then into thick slices
70 ml vegetable oil
3 Tbs aromatic mild curry powder
1 tsp turmeric
1 tsp paprika
1 tsp ground coriander
1 Tbs whole allspice berries

125 g natural sugar
1 Tbs fresh ginger or galangal root,
   peeled and finely chopped
1 Tbs chillies, finely chopped
3 bay leaves cut in strips with scissors
2 tsp sea salt
500 ml white wine vinegar
250 ml water
3 fresh bay or lemon leaves

In Margaret River we used a small fillet of whiting very successfully. You can make a softer pickle by using half verjuice and half white-wine vinegar. Leave the seeds and the veins in the chillies if you want a bit of extra heat.

Method: Cook the fish 2 days ahead of requiring the dish. Pat the fish dry and dip into the seasoned flour. There are some recipes that suggest you should not use the seasoned flour, but just fry the fish in the oil. I prefer to protect the fish from the oil, the pickle makes its way in anyway, and the appearance is prettier. Fry in the hot oil for about 4 minutes on each side or until golden brown and cooked through. As the fillets are cooked, remove and drain on kitchen towels and allow to cool. If desired, the fish can be brushed with oil and baked for about 25 minutes in an oven heated to 180 °C.

Prepare the pickle. Fry the onions gently in the vegetable oil until they are transparent but have not lost their crunch. Add the curry powder, turmeric, paprika and coriander. Fry over gentle heat for a short while to release the aromatic oils from the spices. Add the remaining ingredients (except vinegar, water and fresh bay or lemon leaves) and cook gently for 2 minutes. Pour over the vinegar and water gently to prevent splashing. Over high heat bring to the boil, turn down the heat and simmer the pickle for 10 minutes.

Construct the dish by pouring a bit of the pickle into a glass or china dish. Place a single layer of the fish on top and cover that with pickle. Build up layers of fish and pickle, ending with a layer of pickle on top. Place the fresh bay or lemon leaves on top. Cover loosely and allow to cool completely. When cold, cover with plastic wrap and refrigerate for 2 days. Serve the pickled fish with the marinated onions and a little bit of the sauce.

Wine suggestion: Difficult one this, since you will need a wine that is going to complement the dish. A well-chilled Fantail Rosé from Morgenhof Estate would be a good match. Or a glass of beer.

LEMON MERINGUE CHEESECAKE

Serves 10 slices

This is an adaptation of a recipe that was given me by Mary O'Connor, who ran a bakery in Hermanus where we ran a restaurant called The Burgundy. Mary, who seemed to do nothing but work – hard and all the time – had a bakery and used to bake bread for us, large roundels of white rolls covered with seeds. We used variations of this recipe for the tea we served, and it even found its way on to our dinner menu, flavoured with orange and Van der Hum.

You'll need:

250 g soft butter

4 Tbs castor sugar

4 Tbs sunflower oil

½ tsp vanilla essence

2 eggs for the pastry

1 kg cake flour

4 medium lemons

500 g smooth cottage cheese

2 tins condensed milk

2 egg yolks for the filling

For the meringue topping,
   you'll need:

2 egg whites

125 g castor sugar

½ tsp baking powder

Method: Grease well a 23-cm springform cake tin. Prepare the pastry by creaming the butter in a food processor; add the sugar, oil and vanilla. Add the eggs one by one with a little flour each time to prevent curdling. Add the remaining flour. Press very thinly into the cake tin and chill till firm.

Bake blind at 180 °C until lightly browned and set aside to cool. Turn down the temperature to 125 °C for baking the cheesecake. While the pastry is cooling, prepare the filling. Grate the rind off the lemons, taking care not to take off any of the white pith. Squeeze out the juice and set aside. In a food processor, blitz the cottage cheese and add the condensed milk and lemon juice, blitz again briefly to mix well and add the egg yolks. Blitz again briefly. Pour into the baked pastry case and bake in the preset oven for 20 minutes. Allow to cool.

Now add the topping. Preset the oven to 175 °C. Whip the egg whites until stiff and slowly beat in the castor sugar. At the end, beat in the baking powder and using a spatula spread the meringue on top of the cheesecake. Bake in the preset oven until lightly browned on top. Allow to cool completely and chill before slicing.

Cups of good Assam tea or freshly brewed coffee are perhaps the best accompaniments to drink with this cake.

ADRÉ'S BROWN BREAD

Adré McWilliam-Smith's name should be written in the annals of the history of South African cuisine. She was an unsung heroine who died far too young. Food was her passion and she was way ahead of her time. She had allotment gardeners in Franschhoek growing organic herbs and salad greens for her way before anyone had ever thought of organic in South Africa. Watching her work in her kitchen at Le Quartier Français was a dream. She inspired and taught so many people. As a little tot, our daughter Amy was fed Adré's macaroons and her parents have some wonderful memories of great meals cooked by this special, loved and much missed friend.

Adré taught Maddy to make this bread which she served in her restaurant. She used Nutty Wheat, a flour that was milled in Stellenbosch but is now generally available in South Africa.

You'll need:

1.25 kg Nutty Wheat flour
250 g cake flour
1½ tsp salt
1 cake wet yeast
2 tsp sugar
1 litre lukewarm water

Method: Mix together in a large bowl the two flours and the salt. Crumble the yeast into a cup and add the sugar, add a little luke warm water and stir well. Make a well in the centre of the flour and pour in the yeast. Add the water and incorporate the flour. The mixture should not be too stiff, it should feel soft. Knead for about 10 minutes. Cover and allow to double in bulk – about 1 hour. Knock back and knead briefly. Then split the mixture in two, using a scale to be sure you have equal quantities. Place into 2 loaf tins that have been prepared either with melted butter and flour or with a cooking spray. Cover with a tea towel and allow to double in bulk again – about an hour. Bake at 180 °C for about 2 hours.

This is drop-down delicious bread, well worth the excessive use of arm muscles. Adré had such thin arms too!

RECIPES FOR GREAT PEOPLE

I have had the opportunity to work with some fabulous people and I use this piece to say thank you to them for love given, ideas shared and creating lifelong friendships.

JILL WALSH

Jill came into our lives having read an article about Cape Town in a Dublin newspaper. She had trained and worked at Ballymaloe Cookery School in County Cork and was wanting to travel. She arrived and spent what was for us a very happy time in our kitchen. She was a seriously hardworking young woman with great food ideas. This is her adaptation of a recipe, having seen Madhur Jaffrey making them when she was a guest cook at Ballymaloe.

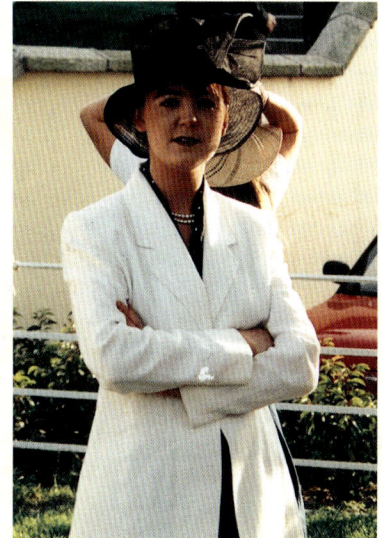

VEGETABLE PAKORAS
WITH THAI-STYLE DIPPING SAUCE
Serves 6

For the batter, you'll need:
180 g flour
1 Tbs ground coriander
1 tsp sea salt
2 tsp curry powder
1 Tbs lemon juice
approximately 250 ml cold water

Method: For the batter, mix together all the ingredients using sufficient water to make a coating batter. Use with aubergine, cauliflower, courgette, mushroom or broccoli to make deep-fried fritters that are served with the dipping sauce. Serve with Thai-style dipping sauce, see page 119.

Wine suggestion: Old Vines, Blue White Chenin Blanc. Irina von Holdt's homage to this grape is a delicious concentration of fruit with elegant minerally overtones.

COMFORT McGREGOR

In the late 1960s, at Lanzerac, I worked with a lady with the blissful name of Comfort McGregor. She had the fastest hands in the business and very seldom worked to a recipe. For speed, and instead of making the caramel that I prefer, she used to melt butter on the bottom of the cake tin and then sprinkle in sticky brown sugar. She never used a recipe and invariably settled on tinned pineapple, incorporating the juice from the tin to soften the cake mixture.

PINEAPPLE UPSIDE-DOWN CAKE FOR COMFORT
Serves 8

You'll need:

1 perfectly ripe pineapple
   weighing about 1.5 kg
250 g butter
275 g castor sugar
150 g cake flour
2 tsp baking powder
3 eggs

Method: First prepare your pineapple. Peel it carefully and cut into rings about 1 cm thick, and cut these into half circles. Using extra, butter and flour a deepish 24-cm cake tin (it's easier to use if it has a removable base). Line the base with greaseproof paper. If you have a non-stick tin, so much the better.

Melt 100 g of the butter in a small saucepan and add 125 g of the sugar. Stir it until the mixture turns a good rich caramel, then pour it into the cake tin, covering completely the sides and base. Arrange the pineapple slices, overlapping slightly, in the caramel on the base of the tin.

Sift together the flour and the baking powder. In the bowl of an electric beater, thoroughly beat the remaining 150 g of butter and the castor sugar till light and fluffy. Add the lightly beaten eggs, one at a time, with a spoonful of flour to prevent curdling and beat well between each addition. Add a little milk if you think the mixture is too thick. Pour the mixture over the pineapple, bang it once on the counter to remove any air bubbles, and bake at 180 °C for 40 minutes, or until a skewer comes out clean. Run a knife round the edge, place a ridged plate – large enough to serve the cake on – on top, turn it (as the title says) upside down and serve. It is more than edible hot, warm or cold.

Wine suggestion: A lovely pineappley, apricoty, raisiny, marmalady noble late harvest, such as Avondale Muscat Blanc or Rouge.

BOUCHARD FINLAYSON WINES

Peter Finlayson is a gentle giant of a man with a tremendous depth of knowledge of his subject. Each experience, from his student years at Stellenbosch University where he graduated as an oenologist, to his studies at Geisenheim, to working in a large winery like Boschendal, to setting up two wineries in the Hemel en Aarde Valley in Hermanus, has added another facet to this multi-layered man.

In his own unique way, he produces probably the finest pinot noir in South Africa from a grape that has crushed many a spirit – indeed, he won the Diners' Club Winemaker of the Year Award for it in 1989. And yet it is in his approach to the wine that his success with it is born. 'I have mentioned that pinot noir is like opera! When it is great it is pure seduction, almost hedonistic. There is no middle road.' You can't fail with a view like that.

Peter produces two versions of pinot noir. Galpin Peak, named after one of the peaks in the mountain barrier that surrounds the Hemel en Aarde Valley, comes out every year. Tête de Cuvée is a limited edition and made only in exceptional years. Both have bold, voluptuous expressions, brushed with excellent oak and filled with the juiciness of cherries, strawberries and the odd little breeze of truffle oil and the gentle presence of ripe tannins.

His chardonnays are legendary and his sauvignon blanc sublime. His Hannibal incorporates sangiovese, nebbiolo and pinot noir – a fusion of Italian and French grapes by a committed African! Hannibal, you will recall, marched his army over the French Alps into Italy using elephants from Africa.

But for me, it is the generous pourings of his Blanc de Mer (white of the sea), with its bracing, salty-savoury, food-countering smack, that hold the best memories. This Peterism is made with a high portion of riesling and splashes of gewürztraminer, sauvignon blanc and chardonnay. It was particularly good while fish and shellfish like crayfish and abalone were being flashed on the barbecue, served with lemon, crispy crunchy salads and warm, home-baked bread. A consummate cooker of fish, Peter has taught me much. 'Take it away from the heat before it is cooked through – it will be cooked to perfection by the time it gets to the table.'

What sage advice, which stood me in good stead in my remaining 12 years as a restaurateur and gave us a name for fish.

My third birthday with my two grannies,
Mabel on the left and Trixie on the right.

ACKNOWLEDGEMENTS

Every single person I have ever met has added to my life experience in some way or another. Some have taught me hard lessons, others have given only joy unconfined and added great lightness.

I am ever grateful to Maureen Barnes, now retired and living with her cat, William, in rural Suffolk, and who got me writing some years back. It was she who talked Alice Bell, then editor of *Fair Lady*, into giving me a regular column. Abigail Donnelly, one of our foremost food writers and stylists, was such a support. Alice's successor, Ann Donald, held my hand too before the magazine stopped its wine column. Much of what is written in this book appeared in *Fair Lady* in some form or another. Other pieces are rewritten from my articles that have appeared in other publications, such as *Indwe*, *Icon* and *Winescape*.

To my many friends in the wine business who have showered me with kindness and unselfishly shared their knowledge – and their product – with me so generously, to the many chefs who have told me their secrets, to many others who have given advice, not always taken – thank you.

My grandparents, Frank Preston, Mary Frances Beatrix and Percy and Mabel Augusta, gave me the anchors I needed as a little boy and many lessons and happy memories that I treasure still, even though almost 50 years have passed since the first of them died.

My parents and stepparents, who I think were more often than not surprised by what I did, were nevertheless always supportive and lovingly uncritical and were the hammer and anvil that forged me.

Thank you Alain Proust for your sensational photography. What a privilege to have one's first book illustrated by this monumentally talented man.

A special thank you to Gorry Bowes Taylor, who pointed me in the direction of Bridget Impey and Russell Martin of Double Storey, to Doug van der Horst who shepherded the project from the time I handed over the manuscript, to Sandy Shepherd, my copy editor, for sensitive changes and sensible word-tweaking, and finally to Petal Palmer – how glad I am to have had a real, professional, award-winning designer like you for this book.

The recipes are all Madeleine's and mine, except where I state otherwise.

Index of recipes

Beef
My bobotie 68

Bread
Adré's brown bread 136
Ultimate cheese and tomato sandwich 86

Cheese
Grilled figs with goat's cheese and
  smoked beef crisp 100

Chicken
Chicken and penne pasta 126
Chicken biriani for Norma 31–2
Chicken breasts with peanut satay
  sauce 130
Maddy's chicken thigh and chick pea
  curry 127

Desserts
Blueberry clouds 111
Galette of fresh dates with caramel sauce 131
Maggie's steamed fruit pudding 73
Malva pudding 72
Mocha mousse for David 97

Nutty Eton mess for Joyce 14
Orange and Van der Hum crème brûlée
  for Hannes 90
Peter Vadas's steamed golden syrup
  pudding 79
Pumpkin fritters 47
Sticky toffee pudding 117

Duck
Duck with blackberry sauce 110

Eggs
Curried eggs for Ina and Ted 58
Frittata for Gabrielle 24

Fish
Cape Malay pickled fish 133–4
Ina Paarman's whole fish over hot coals 57
Pan-grilled calamari tubes on a risotto cake
  with chilli lemon and balsamic
  dressing 116
Smoked snoek pâté 46
Snoeksmoor (braised snoek) 104
Spicy fish cakes with Thai-style dipping
  sauce 119

Guinea fowl
Roast guinea fowl with cèpes risotto 38

Lamb
Sheep's liver in caul 36
Waterblommetjiebredie 105–6

Pasta
Chicken and penne pasta 126
Sauce bolognaise 125
Tomato pasta sauce 125

Rice
Risotto for Giorgio 82
Yellow rice with raisins 70

Samoosas
Samoosas – vegetarian version 107–8

Sauce
Sauce bolognaise 125
Tomato pasta sauce 125

Soup
Boontjiesop (bean soup for Liza) 63–4

Sweets
Pitjie-tameletjies (pinenut and almond
  pralines) 28

Tea eats
Amy and Peter's favourite choc chip
  cookies 87
Granny Nel's cheese scones 54
Koeksisters 20–1
Lemon meringue cheesecake 135
No ordinary carrot cake 88
Pineapple upside-down cake for Comfort 138
Mary McPherson's pendulas 55

Veal
Madeleine's veal stoo 128

Vegetarian dishes
Annette le Roux's pumpkin pie 121–2
Barley and mushroom casserole 49
Boontjiesop (bean soup for Liza) 63–4
Groundnut stew 118
Samoosas – vegetarian version 107–8
Vegetable pakoras wth Thai-style
  dipping sauce 137

Photographic credits
Alain Proust: dustjacket and pages 16, 26, 27, 30, 52, 56, 67, 71, 77, 83, 90, 94 and 106.
Neil Corder: page 69. Jurgen Doom: page 53. Graeme Robinson: page 94.
All other photographs come from private collections.

First published 2005 in southern Africa
by Double Storey Books
a division of Juta & Co. Ltd
Mercury Crescent, Wetton
Cape Town, South Africa
www.doublestorey.com
Reg. no. 1919/001812/06

ISBN 1-919930-87-6

Cover and text design by PETALDESIGN
Edited by Sandy Shepherd
Project management by Douglas van der Horst
Reproduction by Virtual Colour, Cape Town
Printed in Korea by Pacifica Communications